Turning Griping Into Gratitude

A Study In The Psalms

Ron Lavin

CSS Publishing Company, Inc., Lima, Ohio

TURNING GRIPING INTO GRATITUDE

Library of Congress Cataloging-in-Publication Data

Lavin, Ronald J.
    Turning griping into gratitude : a study in the Psalms / Ron Lavin.
        p.   cm.
    Includes bibliographical references.
    ISBN 0-7880-1576-1 (pbk. : alk. paper)
    1. Bible. O.T. Psalms—Study and teaching.   I. Title.
BS1430.5.L38   2000
232'.206—dc21   99-054635
                                                                         CIP

This book is available in the following formats, listed by ISBN:
    0-7880-1576-1   Book
    0-7880-1577-X   Disk
    0-7880-1578-0   Sermon Prep

PRINTED IN U.S.A.

This book
is dedicated
to my daughter, Mary Lavin Cousler,
who sees problems as challenges

and

to Harry and Dodie Andersen
and Roger and Debbie Bise,
who taught this material
at King of Glory Lutheran Church,
Fountain Valley, California

Start All Over Again
by Mary Lavin Cousler

Life is strange. It ebbs and flows;
    it rises and it falls.
When things get tough, it's common to stop;
    it happens to one and all.

But strange as it is, one thing is sure:
    it's up to us every one
To pick ourselves up, dust ourselves off
    and start all over again.

Life is a choice, to win or to lose,
    to lead or follow the crowd.
"Never give up, give in, give out!"
    true leaders shout out loud.

It's easy to hear the words of a jeer
    in place of an uplifting thought,
But deep in the soul the knowledge unfolds
    of good things yet unwrought.

"You're down, you're out, there is no hope!"
    the critics jeer and call.
You feel you've lost, you're done, you're through,
    you're backed up against the wall.

But deep inside you realize
    that it's all up to you.
It's in your mind, the dream, the goal;
    it's yours to make come true.

So when the dark times come to you,
    with all their grief and pain,
Pray and sing; you can beat this thing
    and start all over again.

Table Of Contents

Preface by Jerry L. Schmalenberger   7

Introduction   9

1. Walking Your Talk   17
   Psalm 1:1-3

2. The Secret Of A Right Attitude   25
   Psalm 7:1

3. How Majestic Is Thy Name   37
   Psalm 8:1-9

4. The Shepherd King   45
   Psalm 23:1-6

5. Turning Griping Into Gratitude   53
   Psalm 30:11-12

6. This Fax Is For You   63
   Psalm 27:1

7. Longing For God   71
   Psalm 42:1-2, 5

8. God Is Our Refuge And Our Strength   81
   Psalm 46:1

9. Clean Hearts And Renewed Spirits   89
   Psalm 51:10

10. It Is High Time   97
    Psalm 66:1-2

11. That The Next Generation Might Know   105
    Psalm 78:5-7

12. The Bread Of Life   115
    Psalm 78:11-29

13. From Attractive Distractions To Singing
    Of God's Steadfast Love   123
    Psalm 89:1-2

14. When The World Oppresses You   133
    Psalm 90:1-12

15. My Protector   143
    Psalm 91:1-13

16. Sing To The Lord A New Song   151
    Psalm 98:1-9

17. Your Word Is A Lamp For My Feet   159
    Psalm 119:97-105

18. I Will Lift My Eyes To The Hills   167
    Psalm 121:1-8

19. I Wait For The Lord   173
    Psalm 130:5-8

20. When God Seems Far Away   181
    Psalm 139:1

21. Fearfully And Wonderfully Made   189
    Psalm 139:13-14

22. The High And Holy One Delivers Help And Hope   197
    Psalm 145:13; 146:1-2, 5, 10

23. A Fistful Of Nothing   203
    Psalm 150:1-6

Leaders' Guide   211

Endnotes   213

Preface

The neighbor woman asked me, "... and what do you teach?" I replied, "Homiletics, the art of preaching." She came back with the profound question, "And in your opinion, what makes a really good sermon?" The answer came rolling out with conviction, "A really good sermon for these times:
— is made by a preacher who passionately believes it
— uses simple, compelling, "close to the ground" language
— appeals to the heart as well as the mind
— deals frankly with contemporary life
— extends an invitation
— and always includes an answer to the question, 'So what?' "

These sermons based on the Psalms are "really good sermons" because they meet the above criteria well. One can tell Lavin strongly believes what he writes in simple, close to the ground prose. As in all his former volumes, they are biblically based and come from his big heart, famous in his congregations and communities.

And what an inspiration it is to read homilies which deal head-on with everyday problems and possibilities. The invitation is to join the preacher in the joy and struggle. The concrete suggestions how to respond to such preaching are delightfully obvious.

There is celebration, melancholy, and healing here.

The psalms are so relevant for our day and speak to our troubled souls. God's spirit turns the preaching of them into a congregational event far beyond a lecture on wise biblical sayings.

But then, it's always an event when good friend Ron Lavin mounts the pulpit.

"Neighbor, that's a really good sermon."

Jerry L. Schmalenberger
President Emeritus
Pacifica Lutheran Theological Seminary

7

Introduction

The book of Psalms is the prayer book of the Bible. These passionate prayers demonstrate the many moods of the psalmists —
sorrow and joy,
anger and praise,
grief and happiness,
revenge and kindness, and
griping and gratitude.
It is the counterpoint between this last pair of feelings, which I have chosen as the title of this book. Griping is in tension with gratitude in the book of Psalms and in our lives. The author of Psalm 30 shows both the tension and the resolution to the tension between these extremes when he says, "You have turned my griping into gratitude" (Psalm 73:11, Brandt paraphrase).

The secret of fighting our way through the tension and crossing the river from griping to gratitude is much needed today. Actually, it is not a one-time crossing, but a continual battle to leave the negative feelings of anger, resentment and revenge, fight the currents of cynicism, and find ourselves in the presence of God. Many people not only stay on the negative side of the river, but pass their negative attitudes on to others, murmuring about this or that and dragging others into the muck and mire with them. Griping is a communicable disease, affecting churches, whole communities, even nations.

To turn from griping to gratitude requires the discovery of a secret. It is an open secret. This open secret is a truth frequently found in the Bible, especially the Psalms, but it is not a well-known secret. The open secret is: What gets your attention, gets you.

If you give your attention to your sickness, your anger, your resentments, or your problems, your sickness, anger, resentments,

9

and problems will get you. If, on the other hand, you give your attention to God, God will get you.

The open secret of the Bible is to change your focus from self to God. It is a secret because so few people know it, or if they know it, so few practice it. It is an open secret because it is on almost every page of the Bible, especially the prayer-poems called the Psalms.

E. Stanley Jones, the missionary evangelist, said it clearly years ago. "Whatever gets your attention, gets you. Glance at God and give your attention to your problems, and your problems will get you. Glance at your problems and give your attention to God and God will get you." It is all a matter of focus. On what does your life focus?

The psalmist who wrote, "You have turned my griping into gratitude," (Psalm 30:11, Brandt paraphrase) was sick, maybe even sick unto death, when he found himself in the trap of a negative attitude which gave rise to murmuring and griping. He was still sick when he crossed the river to the land of gratitude. The only thing that changed was his attitude. He gave God all the credit for the change. He did not change himself. He experienced the change. He turned his attention to God with praise and found that suddenly everything looked different. Self-absorption was and is the self-defeating way of the loser. Paying attention to God in prayer and worship is the way to win.

The psalmist had a right to his feelings of discontent. Life had chosen a downward trend for him. Who could blame him for his negative feelings? Sickness makes us feel sorry for ourselves. When friends and relatives disappoint us, who would blame us for holding grudges and griping? Problems took over his mind like a monster conquering a village of pygmies. Problems became the central dominating theme of his life. He could not think of anything else until the moment he discovered or re-discovered the secret of life in worship. He probably began his prayers like this:

It's time for me to worship you again, O LORD, but I
don't feel like it. I know that I shouldn't feel this way,
but everything is going wrong. I'm angry at you for

10

what is happening to me. Things were going so well when ziss, boom, bang, my health broke, my wife started complaining, and my friends and supporters forgot me. Who can I blame but you for what has gone wrong? It isn't my fault. My family and friends have their own problems. I blame you, O LORD.

Then came the turn. The mere mention of God's name must have affected the mind of the psalmist. Suddenly he remembered what he had known all along, but forgot to remember: God is on our side, not against us. Maybe he continued his prayers like this:

O LORD, how foolish of me. It's not your fault that I have all these problems. You love me. You have always been faithful to me, even when I have not been faithful to you. I am sorry for my bad attitude, for my murmuring and my griping. I praise your name. I give you thanks. I am filled with a sense of your wonder and glory. I had forgotten to remember that I am fearfully and wonderfully made and that you are my Creator.

Worship, both private and corporate, does that to us. It shifts our attention from self to God. Perhaps his formerly drooping head and hands were now raised toward the heavens and his words of blame became songs of joy as he sang: "You turned my wailing into dancing.[1] You have turned my griping into gratitude."[2]

Worship is our one hope. Worship, even when we do not feel like worshiping, is our one chance of discovering the secret of the Bible. Worship, even when it starts out with griping, is the one thing needful and the most neglected of all things today. Worship means many things, but primarily it means paying attention to God. When we pay attention to God, we cross the river and find that things look different on the other side. We discover that we are in the land called Promise. God always keeps his word. Therefore we can always start again.

Worship is what Leslie Brandt had in mind when he penned this turn of words — "You have turned my griping into gratitude." Brandt, the author of an inspirational book on the Psalms, died recently. I regret that I never met him, although both of us were ministers in Southern California. He helped me understand and love the Psalms more than he could ever know.

Special thanks go to Harry and Dodie Andersen and Roger and Debbie Bise, who field-tested this material in a class on the Psalms which they taught in 1999. This book is dedicated to them.

This book is also dedicated to my daughter, Mary Lavin Cousler, an author, for the way she describes the turn from the negative to the positive. She frequently says, "Dad, these things that happen to us are not problems. They are challenges."

The challenges of life provide awkward but essential openings for us to turn from self to God through worship. That is the most important turn of all. This turn is called repentance. The Bible is full of insights of people who in the midst of challenges, turned to God for the first time or the hundredth and discovered the land of the living. I am grateful to our daughter Mary Cousler for her helpful reminders of the need for an attitude change through worship.

Every introduction to a book offers acknowledgments to the many contributors to the content of the book. Nothing is original. Any insights you garner from personal or group study of this book come from many sources, some of whom I remember and acknowledge with footnotes, many of which have come to me by watching Christian people live out their lives of worship, service, and witness.

I am particularly grateful for the time off provided by King of Glory Lutheran Church in Fountain Valley, California, to write this book on the Psalms. My associate pastor and partner in ministry, Don McMillan, covered a lot of the work in my absence. Ruth Hancock, Kathy Shutt, and Susan Kiddy, my secretaries over the last ten years when these chapters were written, made many helpful suggestions. Susan did exceptional work on the final draft. You, the reader, will likely find some errors in this book. They are mine. You will also find fresh insights into the meaning of the Psalms. They come from numerous sources.

In addition, Dick Hardel, the executive director of the Youth and Family Institute in Minneapolis, Minnesota, recently reminded me of the creative power of family, both our physical family and the family of God. This emphasis on family is the context of Psalms. The prayer poems in the Psalms are not for rugged individualists, but for people who know their dependence on God and their interdependence on the family of God. We are not soloists, but choir members. We take this journey through life together, not separately. Dick's work with family systems picks up the community emphasis of the Psalms. It parallels my work with small groups.

This book can be used for personal devotions and growth, or as a resource for preachers who preach on the Psalms, but it is primarily aimed at small groups of Christians meeting in homes and churches. These groups need resources, study books which help people learn but also provide openings for discussions leading to growth. At the end of this book, there are suggestions for leaders of small groups. At the end of each chapter, there are discussion questions which will stimulate group participation.

I have written three books about small groups: (1) *You Can Grow In A Small Group* (CSS Publishing); *A Strategy For Renewal* (LCA, Board of Publication), and the most recent, *Way To Grow!*[3], which has questions at the end of each chapter for group discussion. Questions for group use are available for my most recent book, *The Advocate*[4], a book about the Holy Spirit.

The small group movement is one of the most important movements in the church as we begin the twenty-first century. It provides the possibility of congregational renewal through the growth of lay people — who are the hope of the church for the future. Lay leadership development is the heart of church renewal.

Reader, as you consider the continual turns we need to make from griping to gratitude, I hope that you will be enriched by this book and receive support and challenges from fellow travelers in this journey through life.

There are 150 Psalms. Some real gems are not included, but maybe this book will whet your appetite so that you will want to dig deeper into this prayer book of the Bible we call the Psalms.

We read the Psalms for assurance, comfort, and challenge and to find words for our personal prayers. In the Psalms we discover both invitations to firm up our relationship with God and rage at

God for bad things that are happening in our lives; both purpose and confusion; both gratitude found in praise and adoration and griping about a wide variety of discomforts and happenings. In other words, in the Psalms we find a mirror for life.

The Bible quotes in this book are from *The New International Version* (NIV) unless otherwise noted.

Life is like a journey
across
a river.
On the one side
is griping.
On the other side,
gratitude.
Believers cross the river back and forth
many times
always sorry for their griping
until ultimately they cross the final time
and spend eternity praising God.

— Ron Lavin

Chapter 1

Walking Your Talk

---

*Blessed is the man who does not walk in the counsel of
the wicked or stand in the way of sinners or sit in the
seat of mockers. But his delight is in the law of the
LORD, and on his law he meditates day and night. He
is like a tree planted by streams of water, which yields
its fruit in season and whose leaf does not wither.*
— Psalm 1:1-3

* * *

The Psalms are songs of prayer and praise which are intended
to help us in our talk with God and our walk with other people. The
Psalms express our love for God and our work with people. The
Psalms are a guide for both our talk and our walk with God. Psalm
1:1-13 says that this talk and walk can express the law of God.

Talking The Way Of The Lord — Worship
The ancient psalmist says that the man of God is like a tree
planted by life-giving waters. "... His delight is in the law of the
LORD. And on his law he meditates day and night. He is like a tree
planted by streams of water, which yields its fruit in season and
whose leaf does not wither" (Psalm 1:2-3).

Psalm 1 is a song, a sermon, and a prayer. Singing is one of the
most important ways to express our theology. In a survey of church
members on the topic of what is the most meaningful part of worship, singing hymns came out first. By our singing we enforce what
we believe.

Consider the hymn "God Himself Is Present."

*God himself is present; Let us now adore him And with awe
appear before him! God is in his temple; All within keep silence,*

17

Prostrate lie with deepest rev-'rence. Him alone God we own,
Him, our God and Savior; praise his name forever.   (verse 1)

Come, celestial Being, Make our hearts your dwelling, Ev-'ry carnal
thought dispelling. By your Holy Spirit. Sanctify us truly,
Teaching us to love you only. Where we go here below,
let us bow before you. And in truth adore you. "   (verse 4)[5]

Hymns and singing spiritual songs lift our spirits to "higher ground," which the Bible calls God's glory. Singing can help us get above our daily concerns and circumstances. We are lifted out of the mundane to a realm of glory. Singing can put us in touch with the glory of God. J. S. Bach, a Lutheran director of music, wrote next to each piece of music he composed: "To God be the glory." Singing spiritual songs gives glory to God and helps us to realize our purpose in life, which according to *The Westminster Catechism* is "to glorify God and enjoy him forever." When we "talk" God's way through spiritual songs, we are in touch with God's glory. We talk the way of the Lord through spiritual songs. We also talk the way of the Lord through sermons.

Psalm 1 is a sermon proclaiming God's Word and urging people to change their ways. A sermon is not just a speech on a religious topic. A sermon is the Word of God. We need to listen not as an audience, but as a congregation of worshipers. We need to listen for connections with our lives.

Soren Kierkegaard, in his book *Purity Of Heart*, says that the preacher is not an actor on a stage. The listeners' role in a devotional address is not as an audience to judge the preacher's words as being good or bad. The preacher's role is like a prompter, trying to help the actors and actresses on stage with saying and doing the right things. The preacher uses the script which is the Word of God to assist the people. The listener's role is to follow the script which is the Bible. God is the audience who judges how well we do on the stage of life.

The Psalms help us in our prayer talk with God. The book of Psalms is the prayer book of the Bible. Hearing and repeating the Psalms in church and home can help us in our spiritual development. Psalm 1:3 emphasizes that we are like so many trees planted

18

by streams of water. Israel is desert. Most trees planted in the desert, away from water, soon shrivel up and die. The call of this ancient psalm is to stay near to God that we, like trees near a stream, might be nourished by the water of life. Prayer is first and foremost "delighting in God." Sing the words of this Psalm. Say them over and over. Let them become a part of your prayer life.

Worship is the way we talk the way of the LORD — in singing, sermons, and prayers. Psalm 1 also calls us to walk the way we talk.

Walk The Way Of The Lord — Work

Psalm 1:1 says, "Blessed is the man who does not walk in the counsel of the wicked or stand in the way of sinners or sit in the seat of the mockers." This verse deals with walking the way we talk.

Not to walk the way we talk is called hypocrisy. Jesus described the Pharisees as hypocrites (Mark 7:1-8; 14-15; 21-23). They talked one way (very religiously) and walked another way (very judgmentally). When people say, "He talks a good game, but he doesn't walk that way," they are referring to someone who doesn't make the connection between faith and life. Making the connection between what we say we believe and how we act is called walking our talk. Walking our talk means avoiding some things and embracing others. The psalmist lists three things to be avoided.

First, the psalmist says, "Don't walk in the counsel of the wicked." Wicked people urge us to do what they do, namely, to think of self first. Wicked people counsel us to relativize our ethics and rationalize our evil deeds. Wicked people never urge us to do what the Bible says is essential: to repent of our wicked thoughts and deeds. Wicked people urge us to walk in evil ways. The biblical corrective for wickedness is repentance.

Second, the psalmist says, "Don't stand in the way of sinners." The way of sinners is self-centeredness. Sinners stand in the center with everything revolving around themselves. The center of *sin* is "I." The biblical corrective for sinful self-centeredness is to re-center our lives on God.

Third, the psalmist says, "Don't sit in the seat of mockers." Sitting in the seat of mockers has to do with lying, cheating, and mocking good behavior of people trying to walk in God's ways. The biblical corrective for this kind of behavior is to speak well of our neighbors.

We are told what to avoid, namely bad counsel, sinful behavior and wagging tongues which only breed negativism. That is the negative analysis. We are also told what to embrace in order to walk our talk. The two key words for putting our faith into action are "blessed" and "the law of the LORD."

First, Psalm 1 says, "Blessed is the man...." "Blessed" comes from the root verb "to bless." The Hebrew word behind our English translation "blessed" means "to bestow divine favor and confer divine benefits." To be blessed means to be a favored or chosen one. Since God favors you as his child, he expects you to realize that you are blessed and to pass on this blessing to others. As the Bible says, "We are blessed to be a blessing." A blessed person loves God and his neighbor.

Second, Psalm 1 says: "The one who is blessed delights in the law of the LORD." The law of the LORD is summarized in the Ten Commandments. These commands tell us the "do's" and "don'ts" of walking our talk. The Ten Commandments are broken into two sections: (1) what we are to do toward God (the first three commandments) and (2) what we are to do toward our neighbors (commandments four through ten). Jesus summarized the Ten Commandments by describing these two parts in terms of love: "Love the LORD your God with all your heart and with all your soul and with all your mind ... love your neighbor as yourself."

The first commandment says that God is number one in our lives. We are called to embrace God as our highest priority and avoid putting anything else in first place. "I am the LORD your God. You shall have no other gods before me." Embracing this command of God means to keep all false gods from dominating our lives.

The second commandment is "You shall not take the name of the LORD your God in vain." We are called to avoid using God's name in all ways which dishonor God. How many times this past week have you heard God's name taken in vain by idle usage or in cursing? Most people just don't think about their behavior in relationship to this command. We are called to embrace the proper use of God's name which is prayer and worship. God has a name. The way we use it indicates what we think about God. A friend once put it this way: "Contrary to popular belief, God's last name is not 'Damn.' "

Commandment number three says that God has a special day called the Sabbath. What we do with this day indicates what we think of God. "Remember the Sabbath day, to keep it holy," God thundered down from Mount Sinai. Worship is the first priority if we are to walk our talk. Christians are called to embrace the worship of God on the first day of each week, Sunday. In the first table of the law, we are called to avoid beginning each week in any way other than worship.

The second table of the law begins with a reference to home and family. The fourth commandment says, "Honor your father and your mother." The modern home has become little more than a large telephone booth where arrangements are made to leave. This commandment calls us to avoid the tendency in our society to minimize or neglect the family in favor of private priorities, and to embrace the biblical priority of home and family. We are called to act honorably toward parents and restore the family to the second highest place of all, right after God, but not to the exclusion of others.

A bitter man totally misunderstood his responsibilities. Here is what the bumper sticker on his car said: "I love God and my wife. I hate everyone else."

The fifth commandment, "You shall not kill," deals not only with avoiding taking the life of another person, but with hatred and resentment. Jesus interpreted this commandment by saying:

> *You have heard that it was said to the people long ago,*
> *"Do not murder, and anyone who murders will be*
> *subject to judgment." But I tell you that anyone who is*
> *angry with his brother will be subject to judgment.*
> *Again, anyone who says to his brother, "Raca," is*

21

answerable to the Sanhedrin. But anyone who says, "You fool!" will be in danger of the fire of hell.

— Matthew 5:21-22

The sixth commandment is about misuse of our sexuality: "You shall not commit adultery." Adultery means having sex with someone other than your spouse, ruling out premarital and extramarital sex, but Jesus enlarged the meaning to include lust.

You have heard that it was said, "Do not commit adultery." But I tell you that anyone who looks at a woman lustfully has already committed adultery with her in his heart.   — Matthew 5:27-28

The seventh commandment has to do with stealing, taking what does not belong to us. We are called to embrace and have respect for the property of others and avoid the materialism and senseless seeking after more and more toys. A secular man had this bumper sticker on his large RV: "He who has the most toys at the end wins." Wrong!

Commandment number eight, "You shall not bear false witness against your neighbor," means that we are to embrace the good name of our neighbors and avoid the tendency to speak well of ourselves and our motives while mocking, criticizing, and speaking ill of others and their motives.

The ninth and tenth commandments deal with covetousness. "You shall not covet your neighbor's house. You shall not covet your neighbor's wife, or his manservant or his maidservant, or his cattle, or anything that is your neighbor's." The point of these commands is the verb "covet," not the itemized list of coveted items. I once asked a congregation, "Did any of you covet a cow on your way to church this morning?" One man raised his hand and then said loudly: "I have to confess to that sin. I'm a dairy farmer. On the way to church this morning, I lusted after another man's herd of cows." Whether it is cows or property, cars, houses or clothes, the point of these last two commandments is to avoid unhealthy envy of and desire for what belongs to another and to embrace a desire for God which puts all material things in proper perspective. The ancient psalmist offers the biblical corrective for all sin: "Blessed is the man who delights in the law of the LORD and on his law he meditates day and night."

Songs, sermons, and prayers can bring us back to the center of life: love of God which is worship. Avoiding evil people and evil ways and embracing the law of the LORD can help us work for God and discover the meaning of life — love of neighbor which is the only meaningful and lasting work we can do.

Questions For Meditation
Or Group Discussion

1. How did you experience "talk the way of the LORD" (worship through singing, hearing and reading the Word of God and prayer) in your childhood?

2. How do you "talk the way of the LORD" today?

3. What kinds of Christian work, "walking the way of the LORD," do you do today?

Chapter 2

The Secret Of
The Right Attitude

*O Lord, my God, in You I take refuge; save me from all
my pursuers, and deliver me ...*   — Psalm 7:1, NRSV

* * *

Have you had conflicts in your family? Have you ever experienced misunderstandings and accusations from a spouse, a parent, a son or daughter? Have you ever had a family member point an accusing finger at you when you were innocent? If so, this psalm verse is for you.

At work, have you ever had conflicts with your boss or your employees or your fellow workers? Has anyone so totally misunderstood you and your motives that it was difficult for you to go on at work? If so, the psalm verse is for you.

Psalm 7:1 was written in the context of conflict and false accusation. "Yes," someone may be saying, "but under these circumstances ... do you really think that an ancient psalm verse can help me?" Yes, I do. Because this verse raises us from being under our circumstances to being above them by having a right attitude.

The Secret Of The Psalmist Is Having A Right Attitude

There are three ways to deal with conflict: *fight, flee,* or *face* them head on with faith in God. Most folks choose the way of the loser — by fighting or fleeing. The psalmist chose the winner's way, the way less traveled: facing the conflicts with faith in God.

*You know my greatest enemy is myself, how ineffectual
I am in dealing with my inner conflicts. You know, and*

25

*You have assured me that You care. You have judged
my wickedness; now rise up to deliver me from its ugly
consequences.*[6]

This paraphrase of Psalm 7 from Leslie Brandt's book, *Psalms
Now*, a brilliant insight into the way to face conflict while relying
on God as our refuge, clearly shows a salutary change of attitude
which brought resolution to a conflict situation. What was the secret of the psalmist? After much struggle, the psalmist recognized
that the real problem was not out there in what others said or did,
but in his own heart. He moved from self-pity to self-insight and a
new attitude.

In Psalm 7 we have the description of the outward and inner
struggle of a soul before God. The psalmist feels that he has been
wronged by someone. He has been falsely accused. Ever feel that
way? One scholar says that the issue here is that the psalmist was
wrongfully accused of stealing someone else's property.

*He stands charged with theft, yes more, with breach of
confidence in relation to a fellow countryman. The accused has been brought to the Temple and there takes
upon himself an oath of innocence."*— 1 Kings 8:31b[7]

Whether the presenting problem was stealing or some other
conflict, what we have here is the inner struggle of a man who
initially blamed everyone else for his conflicts. It finally dawned
on him that his attitude was contributing to his problem. "You know
my greatest enemy is myself, how ineffectual I am in dealing with
inner conflicts."

It isn't what happens to us in life, but how we interpret what
happens, that determines how we come out. The method of
interpretation is called a right attitude. The psalmist gained a new
attitude.

One pastor described the importance of a right attitude this
way:

*The remarkable thing is we have a choice every day
regarding the attitude we will embrace for that day. We*

cannot change our past ... we cannot change the fact
that people will act in a certain way. We cannot change
the inevitable. The only thing we can do is play on the
one thing we have, and that is our attitude ... I am con-
vinced that life is ten percent what happens to me and
ninety percent how I react to it." — Charles Swindoll

A new attitude — what we need to face life's conflicts, but the movement in this psalm is not just from a negative to a positive attitude. The movement in this psalm and the secret of this psalmist is a new attitude grounded in God, not self, as our refuge.

The Secret Of The Psalmist Is That He
Turned From Self-pity To God As His Refuge

It is a long journey from self-pity and griping to gratitude to God for the lessons learned from life's conflicts, but it is the most important journey of life. The psalmist made that difficult journey as we learn from verse 17: "I will give to the Lord the thanks due to his righteousness, and sing praise to the name of the Lord, the Most High" (Psalm 7:17, NRSV).

The best way to handle conflict is with a positive attitude grounded in faith in God. When that happens, the conflict, or disputed passage as it can be called, can be a point of growth. Sometimes it is only conflict which causes us to find this new dependence on God as our refuge.

In his novel *Disputed Passage*, Lloyd C. Douglas said: "Have you not learned more from those who have disputed the passage with you than all the others?"

The disputed passage where someone is in conflict with you can become the point in life to learn that you may be your own worst enemy. When you discover that secret, you can turn to God in a new way. The secret of the psalmist is that he learned to walk with God and to depend on God in times of conflict and apparent defeat. "I must persist in running to God in my defeats that I may learn to walk with Him in His victories" (Psalm 7:17, Brandt paraphrase).

How do we move from feeling like victims to knowing that we are victors in God? That's the question of a lifetime. That's the

27

question which, when answered correctly, changes our lives. The first step is to accept those things I cannot change.

I cannot change others. I can only change myself. That's the secret of the psalmist — to change himself. We cannot change the attitudes of others, but we can change our attitudes, the way we look at things. The resentment and anger which we feel when we are falsely accused or things go wrong, gets resolved only when we take this first step; then take the second — turning to God. Let me illustrate the secret of the psalmist by three true stories.

Harold was a very athletic young man and did well in school. In fact, in high school he was voted the person most likely to succeed of all his class. But within ten years, he had become a chronic alcoholic and found that, far from succeeding, he was in fact destroying his own life and the lives of those around him. He was jailed in six different states and court-martialed by the Army.

By the end of World War II, Harold had lost most of his faith in God, and had become in his own words an "agnostic," with more doubts about God than faith in God. During this period of time, he underwent much emotional upheaval, the outcome of which was a strong self-hatred. Having nothing to turn to, he decided to kill himself. Before he did it, he thought that he'd better square things with God first.

> *I got down on my knees for the first time in ten years, and I prayed to God for the first time in many, many years. Without fraud, without deceit, and without deception ... my heart cried out in its agony. There was no eloquence in it; there was a cry of despair for help. "God help me. I can't help myself. And if there's any reason for me to live, any reason at all, then take over my life now or let me die. At least let me have the courage to pull the trigger on this gun. And don't stay my hand, because I never want to see another sunrise if I must go on the way I've been going."*

Harold writes:

> *Something happened to me ... I felt something happening deep inside of me, and a peace settled over me that*

28

I had never felt in my life ... I knew deep inside of me
that God had not only heard my prayer, but that He
had answered it and that He would lead me for His
purpose. I knew that I had covenanted with God, that if
He would take over my life and lead me ... that wher-
ever He called I would try to follow ... I got up, un-
loaded the gun and went to bed. I slept peacefully for
the first time that I could remember.

Harold's life had been filled with resentment, revenge, and blaming other people for what was wrong.

These are all self-defeating tendencies centered in an attitude of self-pity. Harold had to learn the basic creed: "I cannot change other people, but I can change myself. I can change my attitude toward a situation by a focus on God who is at work in all situations."

That's how the psalmist discovered the secret of life — by changing what he could change, namely himself, and accepting what he could not change — others. The psalmist saw God as his refuge. He turned from being a victim to being a victor.

In Alcoholics Anonymous, Harold learned the secret of the psalmist which is expressed in what is called the Serenity Prayer:

God, give me the courage to change
those things I can change,
The serenity to accept those things
I cannot change,
and the wisdom to know the difference.
— Anonymous

When Harold began to slip back into the negative attitude of blaming others, a friend challenged him to move toward a more positive attitude. At this time in his life, Harold was a truck driver. He didn't like the laws of the State of Iowa regarding big rigs. "If you don't like the laws, run for office and change them," his friend advised. Harold did just that.

Harold's political career took an unexpected turn in 1957. It marked the beginning of a political career which resulted in Harold's becoming governor of the State of Iowa. Later Harold had a distinguished career as a United States Senator. Still later, in the process of being a viable nominee for President, he suddenly withdrew from the race, and took on the Christian calling of working in prisons with prisoners and other outcasts of society.

Because of his faith in Jesus Christ, Harold began his work with people like he had been, when his attitude was to blame everyone but himself for his troubles. He worked in prisons with outcasts, the incorrigible, the lost, and the damned.

U. S. Senator Harold Hughes was also a key figure in the conversion of Charles Colson, another stubborn sinner caught in the vice of self-pity and pride.

The second story is about Charles Colson. Like Harold Hughes, Charles Colson turned from self-pity to self-insight and repentance before God. As the "hatchet man" in the Nixon administration, Colson at first blamed everyone but himself for the conflicts he was experiencing. As the details of the Watergate scandal began to emerge, Colson at first tried to protect himself.

Senator Harold Hughes and others helped lead Charles Colson on the journey from self-pity and blame to self-insight with God as refuge. It was a very difficult journey at first.

In his own words, here is how Colson responded defensively to a Christian friend named Tom Phillips who tried to help him in the long journey home to God through self-insight:

> *Tom, one thing you don't understand. In politics it's dog-eat-dog; you simply can't survive otherwise. I've been in the political business for twenty years, including several campaigns right here in Massachusetts. I know how things are done. Politics is like war. If you don't keep the enemy on the defensive, you'll be on the defensive yourself. Tom, this man Nixon has been under constant attack all of his life. The only way he could make it was to fight back. Look at the criticism he took over Vietnam. Yet he was right. We never would have made it if we hadn't fought the way we did, hitting our critics, never letting them get the best of us. We didn't have any choice.*[8]

Colson began with defensiveness based on self-pity. He had to move to a new attitude toward God. The change was difficult. He goes on:

> *Even as I talked, the words sounded more and more empty to me. Tired old lies, I realized. I was describing the ways of the political world ... while suddenly wondering if there could be a better way.*
>
> *Tom believed so, anyway. He was so gentle I couldn't resent what he said as he cut right through it all: "Chuck, I hate to say this, but you guys brought it on yourselves. If you had put your faith in God, and if your cause was just, He would have guided you. And His help would have been a thousand times more powerful than all your phony ads and shady schemes put together."*

Tom went on:

> *"Chuck, I don't think you will understand what I'm saying about God until you are willing to face yourself honestly and squarely. This is the first step." Tom reached to the corner table and picked up a small paperback book. I read the title: **Mere Christianity** by C. S. Lewis.*
>
> *"I suggest you take this with you and read it while you are on vacation." Tom started to hand it to me, then paused. "Let me read you one chapter."*

Colson leaned back, still on the defensive, his mind and emotions whirling. Here is what Colson's friend read from the book by C. S. Lewis:

> *"There is one vice of which no man in the world is free; which every one in the world loathes when he sees it in someone else; and of which hardly any people, except Christians, ever imagine that they are guilty themselves. I have heard people admit that they are bad-tempered, or that they cannot keep their heads about girls or drink,*

31

*or even that they are cowards. I do not think I have
ever heard anyone who was not a Christian accuse himself of this vice ... There is no fault ... which we are
more unconscious of in ourselves. And the more we have
it ourselves, the more we dislike it in others.*

*"The vice I am talking of is Pride or Self-Conceit
... Pride leads to every other vice: it is the complete
anti-God state of mind."*

Colson's thoughts and feelings slowly began to change from
defensiveness to openness. Here is what he thought:

*As Tom read, I could feel a flush coming into my face
and a curious burning sensation that made the night
seem even warmer. Lewis' words seemed to pound
straight at me.*

*"... It is Pride which has been the chief cause of
misery in every nation and every family since the world
began. Other vices may sometimes bring people together. You may find good fellowship and jokes and
friendliness among drunken people or unchaste people.
But Pride always means enmity — it is enmity. And not
only enmity between man and man, but enmity to God.*

*"In God you come up against something which is
in every respect immeasurably superior to yourself. Unless you know God as that — and, therefore, know yourself as nothing in comparison — you do not know God
at all. As long as you are proud you cannot know God.
A proud man is always looking down on things and
people; and, of course, as long as you are looking down,
you cannot see something that is above you."*

Colson thought:

*Suddenly I felt naked and unclean, my bravado de-
fenses gone. I was exposed, unprotected, for Lewis's
words were describing me. As he continued, one passage in particular seemed to sum up what had happened to all of us at the White House:*

"For Pride is spiritual cancer: it eats up the very possibility of love, or contentment, or even common sense."[9]

Tom did not succeed that night in reaching Chuck Colson for Christ, but he left him a copy of C. S. Lewis' book *Mere Christianity*. He prayed with Colson and then said, "Let me know what you think of the book."

Later, at a quiet cottage by the sea, Charles Colson picked up the copy of C. S. Lewis' book, saw his pride for what it was, and turned his life over to Christ.[10] He went to prison for his Watergate crimes and there discovered the same attitude of self-pity and pride in other prisoners that had ruined his life. When he was released, Charles Colson began a Christian vocation of helping prisoners turn from self-pity and false pride to God as refuge.

Colson also began to read the Bible as his guide. There he discovered that Saint Paul had made the same long, hard journey to a new attitude of God as refuge.

The third story is about Saint Paul, the Apostle. Saint Paul started out as an arrogant, rude and crude persecutor of Christians. It was a hard journey to conversion with many conflicts within himself and with others. Once converted, Saint Paul still faced serious conflict everywhere he went as a missionary. His own people, the Jews, and the Judaizers among the Christians, opposed him. At one point, some Jewish leaders stoned him and left him for dead. Friends came by and lifted the rocks from him. Saint Paul dusted himself off, and immediately went back to work preaching the gospel of Jesus Christ. How did he do that? He knew the secret of facing conflict by taking God as his refuge. Like the psalmist, Saint Paul was falsely accused of wrongdoing. Like the psalmist, he learned a spiritual secret to bring resolution to his conflict.

Saint Paul describes this secret in two little words he used 164 times in one form or another in his writings. Those words are "in Christ." In Romans 8:1 Saint Paul says, "... There is no condemnation for those who are in Christ Jesus." Conflicts may come, but all condemnations pass for those who are in Christ.

Later in Romans 8 Saint Paul writes: "And we know that in all things God works for the good of those who love him" (Romans 8:28). Conflict notwithstanding, resolution comes to those who love the Lord.

At the end of Romans 8, Saint Paul offers a vision of the biblical secret for conflict resolution.

> *What, then, shall we say in response to this? If God is for us, who can be against us? He who did not spare his own Son, but gave him up for us all — how will he not also, along with him, graciously give us all things? Who will bring any charge against those whom God has chosen? It is God who justifies. Who is he that condemns?* — Romans 8:31-34a

Conflicts and condemnations are seen from an eternal perspective when we take refuge in God. Jesus Christ brings resolution to our conflicts as Saint Paul declares in Romans 8:34b-36:

> *Christ Jesus, who died — more than that, who was raised to life — is at the right hand of God and is also interceding for us. Who shall separate us from the love of Christ? Shall trouble or hardship or persecution or famine or nakedness or danger or sword?*

The psalmist said, "For your sake we face death all day long; we are considered as sheep to be slaughtered" (Psalm 44:22).

Saint Paul rose from being under his circumstances to being above his circumstances as he described the work of Jesus Christ taking us from being victims to victors.

> *No, in all these things we are more than conquerors through him who loved us. For I am convinced that neither death nor life, neither angels nor demons, neither the present nor the future, nor any powers, neither height nor depth, nor anything else in all creation, will be able to separate us from the love of God that is in Christ Jesus our Lord.* — Romans 8:37-39

In Philippians Saint Paul described the secret of taking refuge in God in good times and bad, in times of success and times of conflict.

I have learned, in whatever state I am, to be content. I know how to be abased, and I know how to abound; in any and all circumstances I have learned the secret of facing plenty and hunger, abundance and want. I can do all things in him who strengthens me.

— Philippians 4:11-13, RSV

There are three ways of dealing with conflicts: fighting, fleeing, and facing them. The first two do not work. The third, facing conflicts with God as our refuge and Jesus as our Lord, not only brings resolution to conflicts but turns victims into victors. The biblical secret for facing abundance and want, success and failure, is that we can do all things in him who strengthens us. It happens by a change of attitude.

"Yes, pastor," a stubborn man responded to a pastor's sermon about attitude to overcome hard times. "But under these circumstances...." He then went on to describe in detail how badly he had been treated by life. He repeated, "Under these circumstances...." The wise old pastor interrupted him: "As Christians we are called to live above the circumstances, not under them."

Questions For Meditation
Or Group Discussion

1. What difference has a right attitude made in your life at critical times?

2. What did Senator Harold Hughes learn which changed him?

3. What did Charles Colson learn?

4. What did Saint Paul learn?

Chapter 3

How Majestic Is Thy Name

O LORD, our Lord, how majestic is thy name in all the earth! Thou whose glory above the heavens is chanted by the mouth of babes and infants, thou hast founded a bulwark because of thy foes, to still the enemy and the avenger. When I look at thy heavens, the work of thy fingers, the moon and the stars which thou hast established; what is man that thou art mindful of him, and the son of man that thou dost care for him? Yet thou hast made him little less than God, and dost crown him with glory and honor. Thou hast given him dominion over the works of thy hands; thou hast put all things under his feet, all sheep and oxen, and also the beasts of the field, the birds of the air, and the fish of the sea, whatever passes along the paths of the sea. O LORD, our Lord, how majestic is thy name in all the earth!
— Psalm 8:1-9, RSV

* * *

Psalm 8:1 is a good memory verse for the week ahead of you. It comes from the psalmist's mystical experience of the holy One, including a sense of God's powerful presence in the star-lit heavens and in the psalmist's own soul. The psalmist saw beyond the stars and heard heavenly voices praising God's glory. God's glory has to do with the vertical dimension of our religion.

Our religion consists of two parts — a horizontal and a vertical dimension. These two dimensions make a cross.

This psalm is about getting in touch with the often neglected vertical dimension of our faith here described in terms of glory chanted above the heavens. Glory means radiance and victory.

One night, while under the stars, the ancient psalmist caught a glimpse of the ultimate radiant victory of God. He experienced his inadequacy and smallness as he felt the presence and brightness of God in a glimpse of glory.

He saw behind the curtain of reality to the very mystery and majesty of God, the glorious One. "To God be the glory for the things he hath done," his soul sang. Overwhelmed, he got in touch with God's greatness, his power as ruler of heaven and earth, and God's glory, his radiance and victory over-arching heaven and earth. These words came to his mind: "O LORD, our Lord, how majestic is thy name in all the earth! Thou whose glory above the heavens is chanted."

Glimpses Of Glory

Apparently, three things gave rise to the psalmist's glimpse of God's glory: a baby, the heavens, and a new look at his own soul. First, a child reminded the psalmist of the greatness and glory of God.

In verse two we read: "By the mouth of babes and infants, thou hath founded a bulwark because of thy foes, to still the enemy and the avenger."

Perhaps his wife has just given birth to a baby. Maybe he was out for a night walk after the long process of birth. Thinking about the cries and babblings of a child, the psalmist was overwhelmed by the majesty of God. Maybe he was thinking of the greatness and glory of God as he looked at the baby's eyelashes or fingers or toes. We know he was deeply moved as he heard the baby's cry. Whatever the particulars, the psalmist realized the wonder of it all and thanked God for his power and majesty related to the birth of a child.

The Brandt paraphrase of Psalm 8:2 describes this sense of the glory of God as a baby is born: "Even the babbling of babes and the laughter of children spell out Your name in indefinable syllables."

The psalmist was also thinking of the demonic enemies he faced and how weak they were compared to the God who created new life. The peeps and crying of a baby reminded the psalmist that God is stronger than all the demonic forces around us.

Have you ever gained a new perspective on life, your enemies or problems by looking at the wonder of a new born baby? I have. When I looked at our first child shortly after birth, I was filled with wonder. A child can be an eloquent sermon on the glory of God!

Second, the psalmist was reminded of the greatness and glory of God as he looked at the stars. Let's look at verses three and four:

> *When I look at thy heavens, the work of thy fingers, the moon and the stars which thou hast established ... what is man that thou art mindful of him, and the son of man that thou dost care for him?*   — Psalm 8:3-4, RSV

The heavens declared the glory, the victorious radiance of God, to the psalmist on his nocturnal walk. It was a clear night. There were no man-made lights, only the stars of the skies to illumine his way. As he beheld the sky, he was overwhelmed with the powerful presence of God "whose name is chanted above the heavens."

Has that ever happened to you? Have you ever taken a walk away from the clutter and lights of the city and looked, really looked, at the heavens? If you have, you know how the psalmist felt that night when he wrote Psalm 8. How infinitesimally small we feel when we think about the Creator of heaven and earth.

This great Creator God cares for us! How can this be? He knows each of us by name. He knows our history and our future. He knows our worries and our sins. He knows our down-sitting and our up-rising (Psalm 139:2). The psalmist felt cared for and loved like a child is cared for by a new mother. He sensed the glory of it all as he looked at the bright stars on a dark night.

Third, the psalmist got in touch with the greatness and glory of God when he realized that he was made in the image of God for dominion over creation. Dominion does not mean exploitation, but stewardship.

Yet thou hast made him (man) little less than God, and dost crown him with glory and honor. Thou hast given him dominion over the works of thy hands; thou hast put all things under his feet, all sheep and oxen, and also the beasts of the field, the birds of the air, and the fish of the sea, whatever passes along the paths of the sea. — Psalm 8:5-8, RSV

Other translations read: "You have made him (man) a little lower than the angels." The point is that there is a touch of divinity in us. God has given us the capacity to know him; not only is the glory of God out there in the heavens, but inside, in our souls as well.

Man is made only a little lower the angels, but has dominion over the rest of creation. Dominion does not mean power to use something for our selfish purposes, but stewardship and responsibility for others. The glory of God is reflected in the proper use of our stewardship of the earth and all of its creatures.

Has it ever dawned on you that you are made in the image of God and that you are a part of God's wonderful plan to care for the earth, that you have been given a God-like capacity for caring for God's creation? If so, you have been filled with the awe and wonder which the psalmist experienced. You, too, have discovered the glory of God by discovering the way we are made and the purpose we have as the children of God. You, too, can say: "O LORD, our Lord, how majestic is thy name in all the earth" (Psalm 8:9, RSV).

But there is an even greater reason for us to get in touch with the great glory of God. The psalmist lived before Christ's coming. We have the privilege of living after Christ was born. The brightness of God's glory discovered by looking at a baby, looking at the heavens, and looking at the way we are made in the image of God, is expanded considerably as we look at the coming of Jesus Christ.

The Ultimate Glimpse Of God — In Christ

Saint Luke describes the greatness and glory of God in the person of Jesus in the context of the story of the shepherds keeping their flocks by night. Suddenly an angel appeared and brought them good news of a great joy which was for all people, because a Savior was being born in a stable in Bethlehem. Suddenly the angel was joined by the heavenly host praising God and saying, "Glory to God in the highest, and on earth peace among men with whom he is pleased!" (Luke 2:14, RSV).

God's glory, chanted above the heavens, was revealed on earth in the Savior. God's glory came from beyond the stars to a stable. The presence of God came into our presence.

Saint John describes the glory of God in the coming of Jesus in another way:

> *And the Word became flesh and dwelt among us, full of grace and truth, we have beheld his glory, glory as of the only Son from the Father ... No one has ever seen God; the only Son, who is in the bosom of the Father, he has made him known.* — John 1:14-18, RSV

Stand before this mystery for a moment and you will truly fall to your knees and adore God. The glory of God shines in the person of Jesus. That glory is expanded as we contemplate the wonder of being loved enough that God gave his only begotten Son that all who believe may have eternal life (John 3:16). In the birth of the Word made flesh, we see God's greatness and glory. We see God's victorious radiance even more clearly in the cross.

In the seventeenth chapter of John the glory of the passion and resurrection of Jesus is described in all its wonder. John reports what he overheard Jesus saying:

> *Father, the hour has come; glorify thy Son that the Son may glorify thee, since thou hast given him power over all flesh, to give eternal life to all whom thou hast given him. And this is eternal life, that they know thee the only true God, and Jesus Christ whom thou hast sent. I glorified thee on earth, having accomplished the work which thou gavest me to do; and now, Father, glorify thou me in thy own presence with the glory which I had with thee before the world was made.*
> — John 17:1-5, RSV

41

The greatness and glory of God are revealed in what God did for us on the cross. The power and presence of God came to us in the crucifixion and resurrection of Jesus. The ultimate radiance shines in the darkness as we behold the crucified and resurrected King of Glory.

Saint Paul, reflecting on this glory manifested in the crucifixion and resurrection of Christ, gave rise to praise of God for the wonder of being loved by the King of Glory:

> *As therefore you received Christ Jesus, so live in him, rooted and built up in him and established in the faith, just as you were taught, abounding in thanksgiving.*
> *... For in him the whole fulness of deity dwells bodily, and you have come to fulness of life in him, who is the head of all rule and authority.*
> — Colossians 2:6-10, RSV

Luke, John, and Paul join the psalmist and the heavenly chorus in peeking behind the shroud of darkness and seeing the glory of God. To God be the glory.

A modern gospel song puts it beautifully:

> *To God be the glory. To God be the glory.*
> *To God be the glory for the things he has done.*
> *By his blood he has saved me.*
> *By his power he has raised me.*
> *To God be the glory for the things he has done.*

The psalmist helps us see the bright shining light of the glory of God. "O LORD, our Lord, how majestic is thy name in all the earth!"

Jesus was that glory personified.

Say it out loud: To God *be* the glory. To God be the *glory*. To *God* be the glory.

Questions For Meditation
Or Group Discussion

1. What are some glimpses of God's glory you had as a child?

2. What glimpses of God's glory have you had as an adult?

Chapter 4

The Shepherd King

The LORD is my shepherd; I shall not want. He maketh me to lie down in green pastures: he leadeth me beside the still waters. He restoreth my soul: he leadeth me in the paths of righteousness for his name's sake. Yea, though I walk through the valley of the shadow of death, I will fear no evil: for thou art with me; thy rod and thy staff they comfort me. Thou preparest a table before me in the presence of mine enemies: thou anointest my head with oil; my cup runneth over. Surely goodness and mercy shall follow me all the days of my life: and I will dwell in the house of the LORD for ever.

— Psalms 23:1-6, KJV

* * *

Psalm 23 is one of the favorite passages of scripture for most Christians. It has comforted and assured the hospitalized and the grieving, inspired and comforted the lost and the lonely, and lifted the spirits of the depressed for hundreds of years. It has been used in cathedrals and back alleys, at funerals and in crises, by children and by those about to die. It has enriched the lives of all who have read it and memorized it. Even people who say, "I'm not very religious," generally know the twenty-third psalm. It is personal, as well as communal; it is powerful and it is poignant. Its imagery of a good shepherd with his sheep and of a master of ceremonies at a banqueting table is vibrant.

God Is Our Shepherd

In our urban living, we may have difficulty getting into the rich rural imagery of the twenty-third psalm, but the result of studying this psalm is certainly worth the effort. "The Lord is my shepherd" is a reminder of God's care and encouragement. We like sheep have all gone astray, but the Good Shepherd seeks us out, finds us, and returns us to the flock of God, just as an ancient shepherd in the fields sought out his straying sheep.

A shepherd knows his sheep. He knows what they can do and what they cannot do. He knows that a sheep is not able to take care of itself. It must be in a flock or it will die. Every sheep needs shepherding, caring, and family togetherness. A good shepherd meets the needs and the wants of his flock. "I shall not want" is a magnificent testimony to the extent of caring by the Good Shepherd. Not only our needs, but also our wants are met, as long as they are not in conflict with the purposes of our Shepherd. We can be an utterly satisfied flock of God.

One of our needs is for rest. We need green pastures, places of rest! "He makes me lie down in green pastures," the psalm says. We can work, play, romp, enjoy, struggle, eat, and in our activism, half forget the time-tested truth that rest and peace and quiet are essential to life. Many hospital patients have told me, "I needed this rest." Sheep need to lie down to digest their food. We need to rest to digest all that we take in. We need green pastures — places for withdrawal and digestion.

Another of our needs is for someone to understand our fears. Sheep are afraid of moving waters. "The still waters" are the spots where the shepherd can lead his sheep across the streams and rivers. A good shepherd does not command his flock to cross where their fears would bring panic. He leads them to the quiet waters where he gently stills their fears and helps them cross.

Still another need is for renewal. All of us get tired. All are at times discouraged. All need to be renewed, to be made new again. "Behold, I will make all things new" says the Lord (Revelation 21:5). That's good news. Psalm 23 puts renewal in terms of restoring life from the God who over and over again provides encouragement and the possibility of new beginnings for his people. Sometimes we need new beginnings because we are "cast down."

Sheep can be "cast down," turned over on their backs, unable to raise themselves up. They are pathetic and vulnerable when they are "cast down." They need to be restored by a shepherd or they will die from exposure or from attack. People are like that, too.

We need renewed life. "He restores (revives) my life" means that God gives renewal life to each of us. Life of itself can be lived at a physical, animal level. Food, sex, shelter are all necessities for living. But they aren't enough! We need "life" added to our lives. Jesus said, "I came to give you life, and that in abundance." An extra dimension is added to our lives when we follow the Good Shepherd. As we fail, as we sin, as we are "cast down," we need to be brought back and given life again. As we die, we need what we cannot achieve — life again. It is "life again" which the Good Shepherd gives. Our failures are not final.

We also need to walk the right paths, not the wrong paths of idolatry, immorality, wrong priorities, and attractive distractions. God's right paths, the "paths of righteousness," are advocated in Psalm 23. Wrong paths lead to our personal destruction. We need right paths. "He leads me in the paths of righteousness" refers to right paths where dangers are lessened. God doesn't want us to take wrong paths where certain death awaits us. The path of inordinate sexual passion brings sure death. The path of materialism brings sure death. The path of feeling sorry for self brings sure death. God leads us in righteous paths.

But even taking the right path has its difficulties. While walking the right path, we must go through "the valley of the shadow of death," a valley where we must face the dangers of life and death, and must struggle to survive. Shadowy places are those wherein we cannot see our enemies very well. We need the shepherd to prod and guide us, even when we walk in the righteous paths where God leads us.

The shepherd's rod is a comfort in shadowy places. Literally, the shepherd's rod is a club, a club used to beat off the wolves which attack God's flock. We cannot overcome the enemies in the shadows, but the shepherd defends us, even unto death. "I lay down my life for my sheep," Jesus said. Jesus uses a club to beat off the enemies which would otherwise destroy us.

The shepherd's staff is a comfort for two reasons. First, it is used to keep us in the flock. As we start to stray, we feel the staff on our backsides as a reminder that our life depends on staying together with the flock.

Second, the staff has a crook which can be used to rescue strays, even from dangerous ledges where they have fallen due to their foolish wanderings. You can picture the caring shepherd, leaving the 99 and seeking out the stray sheep. Finding the lost sheep on a ledge of a cliff, the shepherd leans down, gently puts the crook beneath its belly, and lifts it back to safety.

"The Lord is my shepherd" — someone who cares enough to protect me when I am in need, and loving enough to find me when I am lost. The Lord is also the Master of Ceremonies at a royal banquet table at which I am a guest of honor. David, the author of Psalm 23, was a shepherd and a king. Both themes show up in this psalm.

God Is The King; The Master Of Ceremonies

Food, fellowship, and festivity are frequently used in the Bible in describing happiness, even heaven itself. How many times did Jesus say, "The kingdom of God is like a great banquet ..."? God announces good news in this psalm: you are royal guests at the banquet table of the King of the universe. Festivity in the midst of adversity is the theme of part two of this inspirational psalm.

In verse 5 the imagery changes from shepherding sheep to a kingdom banquet for royal guests. In the midst of our enemies, God prepares a banquet. The communion of eating together, of celebrating together, even as enemies are round about us, should be a comfort to us. Who would think of eating at a time like this? "God's people" is the answer. They have God to defend them. With all kinds of problems, troubles, and even enemies assailing us, we go to the banquet of our God to receive the body and blood (the life) of our Lord. We come to the banquet in confidence and faith because the goodness and mercy of our God defend us from our enemies.

"Thou anointest my head with oil," the psalmist wrote. We are sons and daughters of the king, a noble class. The ancient Hebrew custom of anointing royalty with oil is the point of reference. We sometimes think of ourselves as nobodies. God sees the regal nature of his two-footed handiwork. The blessings God bestows upon his noble sons and daughters cannot be contained.

What do you think of when I say, "My cup overflows"? I see a picture of a little thimble beneath a waterfall. We are like thimbles. God's gifts come rushing into us and overflow beyond us. We cannot contain them. God's goodness and mercy are rich beyond description as we stop and think of the gifts which have been poured out upon us.

"Goodness" and "mercy" come from the Hebrew word *chesed* which means steadfast love and faithfulness in God. Whatever your orientation toward God may be — fickle or faithful — his orientation toward you is *chesed* — faithfulness.

"Surely goodness and mercy shall follow me all the days of my life." We had some friends whose little girl used to love to sing the song, "Surely Goodness and Mercy." She would often sing it as she ran and played on the second floor of the family home. Her Christian mother often felt that as she heard the song on the second floor, it was like music from heaven. We live on the first floor called earth. Do you hear the music on the second floor? "Surely goodness and mercy shall follow me all the days of my life ... and I shall dwell in the house of the Lord forever." It is a bright and cheerful experience to hear music and God's encouragement from the second floor of heaven. We can count on God because he keeps his promises.

Earth is the first floor where we live. Do you hear the music and the Word of God coming from heaven? "Surely goodness and mercy shall follow me all the days of my life, and I shall dwell in the house of the Lord, forever."

Think back on your life — the narrow escapes, the near misses, the temptations to which you nearly succumbed. We are precariously situated, flawed, and vulnerable creatures. As we look back on our lives, we realize how important the constant goodness and mercy of God are. Faith is what keeps us from falling. Faith is a gift from God — a response to God's goodness and mercy toward us.

Dwelling "in the house of the Lord" originally meant going to the sanctuary to worship. The larger meaning is caught in the

49

promises of Jesus: "He who believes has eternal life" and "In my Father's house are many rooms ..."

God cares. Like a shepherd, he leads us. Like a king, he holds a banquet for us, his children. Like a loving father, he encourages us. Remember the psalm says that God, the king, anoints your head with oil. That means that the king is our Father and that we are sons and daughters of royal blood.

The Father is on our side. He pays attention to us and makes us winners in life.

A little boy was motioning to a Mississippi River steamboat to come to the shore. "The captain is too busy to notice you," said a passerby. Just then the steamboat turned and started to come to the shore where the boy stood. Smiling the boy said to the stranger, "The captain is my father."

Questions For Meditation
Or Group Discussion

1. Describe God, the Good Shepherd.

2. Describe God, the King who is master of ceremonies.

3. Describe the Good Shepherd/King who is our Father.

Chapter 5

Turning Griping Into Gratitude

You turned my wailing into dancing; you removed my
sackcloth and clothed me with joy, that my heart may
sing to you and not be silent. O LORD my God, I will
give you thanks forever.   — Psalms 30:11-12, NIV

*   *   *

Psalm 30:11 speaks to us of the juxtaposition of deep grief and high happiness. The *New International Version* puts the change from grief to happiness this way: "You have turned my wailing into dancing." *The Living Bible* describes the mood change: "from sorrow to joy." *Today's English Version* describes the mood change of verse 11 like this: "You have changed my sadness into a joyful dance; you have taken away my sorrow and surrounded me with joy."

Elmer Leslie, an Old Testament scholar, says that the meaning of verse 11 is a shift from lamenting wail to dancing delight. [11] He goes on to say that David, the author of Psalm 30, had been sick unto death (verses 1-3 and 9), and now celebrates his restoration with the faithful in worship. Through worship and prayer, David moved from self-consciousness to God-consciousness and thus got into the journey of joy.

Best of all, Leslie Brandt, in his paraphrase of Psalm 30, describes the journey of joy like this: "... You have turned my griping into gratitude." [12] This journey of joy is one which we need to make frequently since we easily get caught in the trap of griping due to circumstances of suffering in a wide variety of forms. Griping is like a communicable disease. When you are around griping, it is easy to get caught in its trap. The journey of joy is a wonderful alternative to the trap of griping.

You can get into the journey of joy by memorizing this Psalm verse and repeating it each day in your devotions this week. It is all about the attitude called gratitude, the opposite of griping.

Griping

Mourning, sadness, and weeping are all part of the human condition. There are times in life when the bottom drops out, things go wrong and we experience "nights of despair." Various translations of verse five of Psalm 30 lift up familiar feelings in terms of night.

We have "nights of despair" (Brandt).

"Weeping may remain for a night" (NIV).

"Weeping may tarry for the night" (RSV).

"Tears may flow in the night" (TEV).

Illness was such a time for David, the author of this psalm. David, the king, had some physical ailment. "You lifted me out of the depths," he wrote (Psalm 30:1-2). In times of illness, sometimes we scream, "Good Lord, where are you?" (Psalm 30:3, Brandt). In such times, we easily fall into the trap of complaining, sarcasm, and griping.

Some people turn away from God and church in times of illness. God doesn't seem to care. We are vulnerable to temptation in times of illness, our own illness and the sickness of a loved one. Illness sometimes leads to mourning, sadness and weeping which sometimes results in griping.

A pastor reports:

> The old man, looking up with imploring eyes, asked me, "What did I do to deserve this? I keep asking myself, what did I do?" All his life he had been active in the church and other benevolent associations. He was the anchor of the congregation for many years — pulling our little church through when it came close to perishing. And now he lay on the bed suffering day and night. "What did I do?" he lamented.

There are no easy answers to the question: "Why do the good people suffer?" Unanswered questions often inspire griping. Illness is like the night, filled with fears and unanswered questions.

Death or near death is also a time of weeping in the night, a time when some cry out, "Good Lord, where are you?" David's near-death experience shook his foundations. He found himself in lamentation, wailing, groaning, and griping. Death or near-death experiences sometimes bring out the worst in us. The fears of the night sometimes produce griping and tears. "Tears come in the night," the psalmist wrote (Psalm 30:5).

1 Kings 17:17-24 also speaks of a situation of tears. A young boy became sick unto death in a time of drought. Elijah, the prophet, appeared. The boy's mother sarcastically said to the prophet: "What do you have against me, man of God? Did you come to remind me of my sin and kill my son?" Prophets are called to preach. "We don't need any preaching here," the mother was saying. Prophets are called to judge. "We don't need any judgment here," she was saying. Caught in the web of the negative attitude of griping, the widow's response to her son's sickness was to complain bitterly out of guilt and fear. With no one else to blame, she blamed herself. "Did my sins cause this?" she asked. She also blamed the prophet Elijah and God. This is a familiar scenario.

Illness, death, or near-death experiences are all times of grief. Loss of any kind can lead to grief. The experience of loss can lead to griping.

Lutheran theologian Granger Westberg puts it this way: "All loss is experienced as grief."

All loss —
loss of health;
loss through death of a loved one; or your own near death;
loss of a friend;
loss of child in the "empty nest" years;
loss of a job;
loss through moving to a new location;
all loss is experienced as grief.

Grief can turn to groaning; groaning to griping. Be careful of the grip of griping. It can become a way of life. Saying negative things at negative times is better than keeping it all in, but some people stay on the negative note for life. Griping feeds itself. Griping worsens an already bad set of circumstances. People thus cut themselves off from the very sources that would help them — God, church, family, and friends. Some people seem to make a habit of griping. Griping becomes a way of life. Some get caught in the grip of griping and never get out. David found a way out. He moved from griping to gratitude, overcoming his sense of loss.

Loss means a feeling of being dislocated, of being placed in an unnatural place where we feel lonely, awkward, and dependent. Unless we are careful and prayerful in times of dislocation, we can get caught in the trap of a negative attitude.

Consider these words about dislocation:

Reflections On Being Dislocated

Moving is an experience of dislocation.
    Nothing is familiar.
Old friends are gone. Old supports are not there.
A person feels out of place when there is a new location.
    A person feels dislocated.
The same thing happens when sickness comes, or death.
    Something is wrong. Something is out of place.
There is a hole in one's soul,
    even when God has been close in the past.
The feeling is that you are dislocated;
    you are not where you ought to be.
Chances are, you have experienced both of these dislocations
    in your life.
When faith is mature and the Christian can hold on
    in these times of dislocation,
      there is the possibility of a new awareness of God.
That awareness means that we discover or re-discover
    that our location is with our Maker.

                             — Ron Lavin

When we are dislocated, we can no longer trust in our own strength. In this circumstance we can learn to trust God in a new way. David trusted in his own strength until "God hid his face" (Psalm 30:7). Then the bottom dropped out and he had to learn to depend on God. David, the psalmist, turned in on himself with the loss of self-confidence. In misplaced self-confidence he found only misery. Murmurings proceeded from his heart and mouth. Loss does that to us. In the case of David, the move from griping to gratitude was not just a matter of the healing of his body. It was also a matter of the healing of his attitude. In times of prosperity he felt invincible. That was part of the sickness — an attitude of griping based on a feeling of being invincible, which came out of self-centeredness.

"When I felt secure, I said, 'I will never be shaken' " (Psalm 30:5). In a time of adversity and dislocation — sickness, near-death and loss — David found his security in God, not self, and his health was restored. He moved from self-centered griping to gratitude to God.

Gratitude

In his new found gratitude the psalmist wrote: "Weeping may come in the night, but rejoicing comes in the morning" (Psalm 30:5). That journey from night to day was an attitude change from griping to gratitude. Many of us get caught in the grip of griping when things go wrong. We need the attitude change described in Psalm 30:11 (Brandt paraphrase): "You have turned my griping into gratitude."

The move in mood from anger and self-pity to gratefulness is the move of a change of attitude through prayer and worship. What took place was a reversal in David's attitude.

Sometimes the attitude of griping is picked up because there is a lot of griping around us. That happened to me in 1975 when I was a delegate for the Lutheran Church in America to the World Council of Churches meeting in Kenya, Nairobi. Christians from all nations met in this African city to consider the weighty issues of the world and the churches. Many of the speeches were anti-American. "America had too much power, too much influence, too much money," delegates said. At first I was defensive about my country. Then, little by little I picked up on the criticism. After all, there were some partial truths in what was being said.

When I returned to America, I saw the Statue of Liberty as we descended for a landing. That made me re-think the criticisms I had heard and repeated. When I returned to my home in Davenport, Iowa, Forrest Kilmer, the editor of the local newspaper, asked me to write an article about my trip. I titled the article: "What Is Right With America." I emphasized three freedoms in the article. First, we have freedom of speech. Most of the other countries from whom criticism of America had come had a controlled press. For example, the newspaper in Kenya was little more than a publicity bureau for the government.

Second, we have freedom of movement. In many of the countries of the world, you could not move freely from place to place. You had to get permission from the government to move. Often this permission was delayed for months and then denied.

Third, we have freedom of religion. That means that we can worship as we choose. Many delegates from around the world reported that the government severely limited and in some cases persecuted them because they were Christians. I concluded the article by saying that my attitude had changed from griping about what is wrong with America to being very grateful for being an American. That is the movement which we see in Psalm 30.

A missionary tells the story of how he turned from griping to gratitude as he served in Brazil. The twin devils of anger and self-pity threatened him as he dealt with airline schedules, a video camera, and car troubles. While taking some relatives to the airport, he discovered that their flight was canceled. No warning, no explanation. Just a cancellation which left everyone stranded.

After a long wait, the missionary decided to do something productive on the way home. He took out his video camera and tried to record a spectacular waterfalls area. The trouble was that it was raining. Then he realized that he had left his video camera turned on for the previous hour and that the battery was dead. When he got back to the hotel, he realized that the rain had ruined his camera. It cost him 300 dollars to get it fixed.

Later that week, his new car, the one that the car dealer said was worth the extra money, would not start. He called a mechanic. "Yes," he said, "we will send the tow truck to pick up the car in a few minutes." Hours later, as the tow truck arrived, the missionary tried the ignition one more time. The car started. Of course, the tow truck driver insisted on being paid. "Was it my fault that your car started?" he asked sarcastically.

The twin devils of anger and self-pity moved in like a fog in the mind of the missionary. He was in a foul mood when a nine-year-old boy, shirtless, bare-footed, and dirty, knocked at the window of his car at a stop light. "Do you have any spare change, sir?" the boy asked. He and his friends were hair-matted, skin-crusted and homeless street orphans. "How much have you collected today?" the missionary asked. The dirty hand opened and showed a few coins.

The missionary, with tears in his eyes, opened his wallet and offered the equivalent of a dollar. The twin voices of anger and self-pity took a back seat to the presence of God when the missionary realized the difference between his frustrations over airline schedules, a video camera, and his car and the boy's frustrations over not having a meal and a place to sleep at night. The boy was an angel from God sent to wake up the man of God to change his attitude from griping to gratitude.[13]

That is what happened to David. The night of self-centeredness passed and the dawn of God's presence appeared. David's attitude changed as he prayed and worshiped his Maker. Nothing else changed but his attitude, but that was a big change — from griping to gratitude. This change from griping to gratitude is called the reversal.

The reversal is a journey into joy, a change from night to day.

Leslie Brandt helps us see the possibility of the reversal in our attitudes.

> *I am up a blind alley, Lord.*
> *The props have been knocked out beneath me.*
> *I feel as if I'm grappling with the wind*
> *   for some support or security.*
> *I've been pulled up short, Lord.*
> *Now I realize how much I need*
> *   something or someone*
> *   beyond and above myself*
> *   to give stability to my tenuous existence.*[14]

The psalmist of old had many of the same problems which we experience today. Illness, death or near death, and loss often lead to anger, self pity, self-centeredness, and griping.

The psalmist experienced griping and weeping in the night, but in the great reversal, testifies of a special gratitude he learned as he turned to God: "Weeping may tarry for the night, but joy comes in the morning" (Psalm 30:5, RSV). "You have turned my griping into gratitude" (Psalm 30:11, Brandt).

A retired Christian was recently told by his doctor, "You have cancer." "How long do I have to live?" the man inquired. "Probably about five years," said the doctor. "Surgery in this case won't work." "What do I do?" "Well," said the doctor, "you can spend the next five years with one of two companions, griping or gratitude. It's up to you."

Which will it be for you? You've got only a limited time to live. Whether you spend it in lamenting or living, griping or gratitude, is up to you.

Questions For Meditation
Or Group Discussion

1. "All loss is experienced as grief." Do you agree or disagree? Explain.

2. Describe times of dislocation

   • in your childhood:

   • in your adult life:

3. What are some of the outward evidences of griping and gratitude?

   • griping:

   • gratitude:

Chapter 6

This Fax Is For You

The Lord is my light and my salvation — whom shall I fear? — Psalm 27:1

*   *   *

There will be a test at the end of this chapter. Please read carefully so that you can give the right answers.

Psalm 27:1 is about what happens when God finds us. The psalmist wrote this message about 3,000 years ago, but it comes to us today in powerful and personal ways. This message from long ago is true, but does it make a difference for you?

Recently, one of our church secretaries handed me a piece of paper and said, "Pastor, this fax is for you." The fax came from St. Paul, Minnesota. Minnesota is many miles away from Southern California. The information in the fax was about some important business of the church. That made me think about another important message that has come from a greater distance: "The Lord is my light and my salvation."

The psalmist received this message and passed it on with a sense of urgency many years ago. The message is timely in our day too. Psalm 27:1 is a good memory verse for this week. You will find that it helps you in ways that are powerful and personal. As the secretary said, "This fax is for you."

The Message Of Light Is For You Today

The original context for this verse is the darkness of intrigue and evil-doing on the part of the enemies of the psalmist (Psalm 27:2). We don't know what they did, but it felt like a whole army was encamped against him (Psalm 27:3). Then he remembered the words he had heard from deep within his soul: "The Lord is my light ... whom shall I fear?"

There is a new "No Fear" logo which has emerged in the last several years. You see it on shirts and bumper stickers. The secular concept behind the logo "No Fear" is that we can be strong enough to put down all fears. Recently I saw a bumper sticker which is a biblical corrective to the secular slogan. "Have no fear. I am with you always." This biblical corrective exposes the false bravado of self-centered courage based on our own strength. It also shows that believers can move through the darkness because God who is with us sheds light wherever we go. "Let there be light," God says for your life pilgrimage and mine. We respond, "The Lord is my light."

The Bible uses the imagery of darkness and light to announce and share the good news that the light of God comes to us, and we should let it shine through us. The creation story is about light overcoming darkness. Darkness covered the earth. Then God said, "Let there be light" (Genesis 1:3). The prophets brought the light of God to the people who dwelt in great darkness. 1 John 1:5 says, "God is light and in him is no darkness at all."

The Word of God comes to us. That Word is life and light. The Gospel of John reports it this way:

> *In the beginning was the Word, and the Word was with God, and the Word was God. He was in the beginning with God. All things came into being through him, and without him not one thing came into being. What has come into being in him was life, and the life was the light of all people. The light shines in the darkness, and the darkness did not overcome it.* — John 1:1-5

Jesus describes his mission in terms of light overcoming the darkness. "I am the light of the world. Whoever follows me will never walk in darkness but will have the light of life" (John 8:12). Jesus also said, "You are the light of the world" (Matthew 5:14). The light of God comes to us in Jesus Christ. Then it shines through us to the world.

How does this message of light over darkness play out in your life? We are called to come into the kingdom of light. Sin is a matter of dwelling in darkness. Selfishness or self-centeredness holds you in bondage and darkness. God's light over darkness calls for a renunciation of sinful motivators, because as Jesus says, "The kingdom of heaven is near" (Matthew 10:7). Let me put the message of the heavenly light of the kingdom of heaven breaking into life today into the context of a real life story.

John was an agnostic for most of his adult life. "John is one of the best lawyers in town," a mutual friend said about John. "He is tough, stubborn, and strong-willed. He doesn't believe in God, and he wants no part of church, but if you ever need a lawyer, he's your man." I met John many years ago when he was a member of the same YMCA in Davenport, Iowa, where I played racquet ball. Several men from the Y started a new study group called a *koinonia* (fellowship) group. John was invited to join us as we read and discussed *The Cost of Discipleship* by Dietrich Bonhoeffer. Men in that koinonia group did a lot of genuine sharing and witnessing to the lordship of Jesus Christ and the kingdom of heaven. Several lawyers, businessmen, and a psychiatrist met with me weekly to talk about discipleship. The sharing by the laymen in that group resulted in John's rethinking his lack of belief. John was converted. I baptized him on March 7, 1976, at St. Paul's Lutheran Church in Davenport, Iowa. The light of God broke into John's darkness. John became a disciple of Jesus Christ. The kingdom of heaven broke into his life.

John had been a World War II pilot. He was shot down. For a long time John carried the burdening question, "Why was I kept alive when my friends were killed in a crash on August 21, 1944?" On August 21, 1992, 48 years to the day from the time of the plane crash which began John's spiritual journey, John's funeral was held at St. Paul's Lutheran Church in Davenport, Iowa.

This unusual timing is matched by the timing of one of the devotionals in a booklet produced by St. Paul's Lutheran Church where John was a member and leader. The message for the week of John's death was based on Isaiah 42:16:

I will lead the blind by a road they do not know, by paths they have not known I will guide them. I will turn the darkness before them into light, the rough places into level ground. These are the things I will do, and I will not forsake them." — Isaiah 42:16, NRSV

"The devotional for last week was written by my father based on Isaiah 42:16," John's daughter Martha said on the phone when she called to tell me that John had died of colon cancer. "You changed his life," she said, "and through Dad the lives of many people in our family were changed." "It wasn't me, but Christ," I said. "Yes," she replied, "but you and the people in his group witnessed to Dad and helped him become a strong Christian. He in turn brought light to others."

The light of God comes to us. It also shines through us. John not only came into the kingdom of light. He shared that light with others. The Bible puts it this way:

You are a chosen race, a royal priesthood, a holy nation, God's own people, in order that you may proclaim the mighty acts of him who called you out of darkness into his marvelous light. — 1 Peter 2:9

Yes, but more workers for the kingdom of light are needed if we are to reach the dark world with this message of light. As Jesus said, "The harvest is plentiful but the workers are few. Ask the Lord of the harvest, therefore, to send out workers into his harvest field" (Matthew 9:37-38). Jesus also said, "Freely you have received, freely give" (Matthew 10:8).

Is this fax for you? Let me put it another way.

The Message Of Salvation Is For You
The original context of our psalm verse was spiritual blindness, ethical crookedness, and moral perversion. The psalmist felt that his enemies were setting traps for him, falsely accusing him and slandering his reputation. He felt the harsh blows, bitterness, and divisiveness of his adversaries. That is why the word "salvation"

is so important. Salvation means wholeness and togetherness. "The Lord is my salvation; whom shall I fear?" the psalmist wrote.

The Bible uses the word "salvation" for this life and the next. In this life, salvation means victory over one's enemies, health over sickness, and freedom from the fear of hostile powers. Salvation is for the here and now. Salvation means that the divisiveness around you and within you is put to flight. When the light of salvation shines on you, you must make a choice to accept it or reject it. Consider three action words of response as you consider your response to the light of salvation shining on you: *save, choose* and *ask.*

Save: Peter in his great Pentecost sermon puts it this way: "Save yourself from this crooked generation" (Acts 2:40). Is there any doubt about the crookedness of the generation in which we live? With morality on the decline, secularism on the increase, and violence, drugs, and alcoholism on the rise, Peter's words about the crooked generation ring true. We need to hear a word of hope. We need to choose sides and firmly fix our feet on the winning side. "The Lord is my salvation," the psalmist wrote. What difference does salvation make for you today?

Choose: As Joshua said in his day, "Choose this day whom you will serve. As for me and my household, we choose the Lord." "The salvation of heaven is near," Jesus said. Salvation is for the here and now. It means wholeness instead of being caught up in the divisiveness of our surroundings. If we accept the light of salvation when it comes near to us, we then become the instrument of God's light. "You are the light of the world," Jesus said (Matthew 5:14). The light of salvation comes to us; then it goes through us to others if we make the right choice.

Ask: Ask yourself this question: "Does the light of God shine through me? Am I a builder or a wrecker?"

An unknown author put it in this way:

> *I watched them tearing a building down*
> *A gang of men in a busy town.*
> *With a ho-heave-ho and a lusty yell*
> *They swung a beam and a side wall fell.*

I asked the foreman, "Are these men as skilled
As the men you'd hire if you had to build?"
He gave a laugh and said, "No indeed —
Just common labor is all I need.
I can easily wreck in a day or two
What builders have taken a year to do."

I thought to myself as I went my way
Which of these rules have I tried to play?
Am I a builder who works with care
Measuring life with rule and square?
Am I shaping my deeds to a well-laid plan
patiently doing the best I can?

Or am I wrecker who walks the town
Content with the labor of tearing things down?

When we confess "the Lord is our salvation," we are choosing the role of a builder instead of a wrecker in the here and now. But salvation is more than just for the here and now. It also includes the hereafter. Salvation has to do with people finding a living relationship with God which has results in the life to come, the kingdom of heaven in its fullness.

Let me put it in story form. A young man named Charles was sitting in a pew one day in 1850, just as you do on Sundays. He had been around church for a long time, but the light of salvation had never dawned on him personally. He had never made a commitment to the Lord. That is true for many today too. They have never personalized the message of salvation. The regular preacher for the day was sick, so a layman got up and gave the sermon. There was no great eloquence in it, but the sermon was on a great text which changed Charles' life. The text was Isaiah 45:22: "Turn to me and be saved, all the ends of the earth! For I am God and there is no other."

Thus began the career of Charles Spurgeon, one of the greatest preachers in the nineteenth century. The light of salvation came to him. He embraced it. Then it started to shine through him. Spurgeon addressed thousands upon thousands of people in his preaching this message: "Turn and be saved." Many came to faith in this life and received peace for the next life because of this simple message of salvation: "Turn to the true God; no other god will do." The light of salvation came to Spurgeon; then it shined through him.

Jesus said, "I came that they may have life, and have it abundantly" (John 10:10). Salvation means abundant life in the here and now and eternal life in the world to come! Jesus also said, "I go to prepare a place for you" (John 14:2). Will you have a place in eternity? That depends on your response.

A sermon should be judged on two counts: (1) Is it true? And (2) Does it make a difference? This Word of God is true. "The Lord is my light and my salvation" (Psalm 27:1). Does it make a difference? That is up to you.

Your earthly life is not forever. Where will you spend eternity? The Word comes across time and eternity. "The Lord is my light and my salvation."

The test I promised you at the beginning of this chapter has two questions:

(1) Is this fax for you?

(2) How will you respond?

Questions For Meditation
Or Group Discussion

1. When you think about light, what comes to mind?

2. How does the story of John in this chapter connect with Psalm 27:1?

3. How does the story of Charles Spurgeon connect with Psalm 27:1?

Chapter 7

Longing For God

As a deer longs for flowing streams, so my soul longs for you, O God. My soul thirsts for God, for the living God. When shall I come and behold the face of God? Why are you cast down, O my soul, and why are you disquieted within me? Hope in God; for I shall again praise him, my help and my God.

— Psalm 42:1-2, 5, NRSV

* * *

Some years ago my wife and I were on vacation visiting a friend named Lois who had lost her husband Lou, a medical doctor, a short time earlier. Lou had died quite suddenly while out jogging one morning. We had been close to this family for a long time. It was good to see Lois again. We stayed with her in her new home on the Monterey Peninsula in California. When Lois discovered that we were celebrating a wedding anniversary while we were there, she said that she and her sister would like to take us out to dinner. The dinner was at the restaurant and clubhouse of Pebble Beach Golf Course, one of the most picturesque golf courses in the world.

As we ate dinner overlooking the eighteenth green of Pebble Beach Golf Course, Lois asked if I played golf. "I love the game," I said, "but I don't get out very often." Lois' sister asked, "Would you like to play tomorrow here at Pebble Beach?" That is like asking a baseball fan if he would like to play baseball at the World Series. "That would be wonderful," I replied, "but isn't it very expensive?" "You will be our guest," the sisters replied.

The fairways were clean and beautiful, like a carpet. The undulating greens were manicured like none I had ever seen. The view overlooking the cliffs and crashing waves of the ocean was magnificent. I was really impressed with Pebble Beach Golf Course. But what impressed me more than anything else was the sight of the deer. We saw deer on almost every hole. We saw over 100 deer grazing and running around the course and stopping for a drink that day. It was a sight never to be forgotten. The amazing experience of the deer on the Pebble Beach Golf Course reminded me of Psalm 42:1, "As a deer longs for flowing streams, so my soul longs for you, O God."

Deer long for water. We humans long for God. God created us. All of life is a search to return to God, but we sometimes get diverted by trivial pursuits.

Trivial Pursuits

Trivial pursuits are those longings we substitute for the longing for God. They include the pursuit of money, fame and things. They include a distorted love of sports or clothes, cars or boats. They include seeking after bad things to the neglect of God. They even include seeking after good things to the neglect of God. Bad things and good things are exposed as trivial pursuits when we discover God in the context of extreme circumstances.

Saint Patrick of Ireland wrote about the lesson on the deer's longing for water, pointing to our longing for God as the ultimate pursuit in life. Like the psalmist in Psalm 42, Saint Patrick had to rise above circumstances and the trivial pursuits of the world. The life of Saint Patrick and his ability to rise over insurmountable odds, bears witness to the power of the God in whom he put his trust.

Patrick was born about A.D. 414 near the western coastline of the Roman province of Britannia, most likely near the shortest sea route from England to Ireland, opposite Ulster. This would place his home somewhere between the Antonine Wall and Hadrian's Wall.

When Patrick was only sixteen, he was captured by a raiding party from Ireland and sold as a slave to a petty king in Armagh. In an instant, the privileges of home, securities of position, and plans for the future were gone. It would have been easy to despair, to curse God and ask to die; but this is the time when Patrick's faith, and his personal relationship with God, were greatly strengthened. In his *Confessions* he writes:

> *After I came to Ireland — and so tended sheep every day, I often prayed in the daytime ... up to a hundred prayers and at night nearly as many and I stayed in the forest, and on the mountains and before daylight I used to be roused to prayer in snow, and in frost and rain, and I felt no harm, nor was there any inclination to take things easily in me, because as I see now the Spirit seethed in me.*

Through constant prayer Patrick built his living relationship with God. He knew he was not alone; and he triumphed, not in his own might, but in the power and presence of God. "The Spirit seethed in me" is Patrick's way of expressing his love for life and for God.

Patrick's faith helped him not to lose hope. Often he dreamed of escape. After six years the opportunity came, and he returned home to England. But Ireland had already captured him. He had dreams in which he seemed to hear his friends and the Irish calling to him: "We pray thee, boy, to come and henceforth walk among us." In spite of pleas from his kinsfolk, and the dangers of being put to death as a runaway slave, Patrick was determined to return as a missionary to Ireland.

He reached Ireland again in about 455. In his *Confessions* he gives as his reason for returning — he needed to expiate the sins of his youth by preaching the gospel in Ireland. There is no doubt that the driving force behind Patrick's return was the Living God. Patrick speaks of his faith as an inner experience: "And another time I saw Him praying inside me as it seemed ... so I believe! — because of His indwelling Spirit, which has worked in me ever since that day."

Patrick relates how he met Christians on his travels in Ireland even in remote regions "where no-one had yet come to baptize." Later he went to Gaul for training and ordination. This time when he returned he came to Tara, "the centre of witchcraft and idolatry in Ireland." Here was a test for Patrick and the future of Christianity in Ireland; here the new religion would confront the old ways of idolatry.

When Easter approached, Patrick was determined to keep the festival in Tara. The feast of the Risen Lord was a time to rise over the heathen. As it happened, Easter coincided with a great pagan festival at Tara. All lights were to be extinguished and all fires put out. According to pagan tradition, only the king could provide people with light and fire. Patrick and his companions pitched their tent, collected wood, and kindled the Pashal fire, which lit up the whole area around Tara. The king's men warned the king that unless the fire was extinguished immediately, it would spread everywhere in Ireland with its light. Speaking of Patrick they warned the king: "He goes around the Munster men and preaches to them and baptizes them and leaves them clerics and churches. This is he of shaven head, the falsifier who is deceiving everyone. Let us go and attack him and see if his God will help him."

The king had no doubt that Patrick had to be stopped. He said, "We will go and slay the man who has kindled this fire." Soldiers were sent to capture Patrick and prevent him from leaving the area. They surrounded him and his men. When Patrick saw them, he quoted the Bible: "Some put their trust in chariots and some in horses; but we in the Lord our God." He escaped his attackers, came to no harm, and entered Tara itself.

In the eyes of the people there was no doubt that the power of this new religion was greater than the religion of the pagans. Legend grew that Patrick, one of the first Celtic Christians, was more powerful than the pagan priests called Druids, that he was a "shape-changer." Tradition says that this is when he composed the hymn known as "The Deer's Cry."

In the poem called "The Deer's Cry" Saint Patrick wrote about Jesus:

> *Christ be with me, Christ within me,*
> *Christ behind me, Christ before me,*
> *Christ beside me, Christ to win me,*
> *Christ to comfort and restore me,*
> *Christ beneath me, Christ above me,*

Christ in quiet, Christ in danger,
Christ in hearts of all that love me,
Christ in mouth of friend and stranger.

"The Deer's Cry" expresses so well much of the early
Celtic Christian faith. It vibrates still with the God who
surrounds us, the Christ who is with us and the Spirit
within us ... It is a mystery to be enjoyed, not a problem
to be solved. Saint Patrick urges us to set out to enjoy
God, his Presence and Power.[15]

Saint Augustine also wrote about the Presence and the Power of God. He described the longing in the human heart for God which easily gets diverted to the unsatisfying search for other things. Before he became a Christian, Augustine got caught in the web of searching for learning as an ultimate goal. He also got caught in the web of lust, having an illegitimate child. When he became a Christian, Augustine wrote: "Lord, our hearts are restless until they rest in Thee." When he became a Christian, Augustine saw all worldly drives as trivial pursuits compared to finding rest in God.

Blaise Pascal in his book *Pensees* describes the distractibility of people from God and prayer like this: "When I occasionally set myself to consider the different distractions of men ... I have discovered that all the unhappiness of men arises from one single fact, that they cannot stay quietly in their own chambers."[16]

Pascal shows the difference between earthly things and things eternal and how we are so easily lured into majoring in minors: "It is not to be doubted that the duration of this life is but a moment; and that the state of death is eternal, whatever it may be."[17]

Pascal observed the double nature of the human being who can seek after God like the deer longing for water or go after a wide variety of trivial pursuits which only get him into trouble:

What a chimera then is man. What a novelty! What a
monster, what a chaos, what a contradiction, what a
prodigy! ... Judge of all things, imbecile worm of the
earth, depository of the truth, a sink of uncertainty and
error, the pride and refuse of the universe.[18]

75

We were created to seek God like a deer seeks the waters of a brook on a foggy morning. Instead, we often seek something else and make it into a false god which only hurts us.

The Longing For God

In the context of a temporary depression, the psalmist speaks of resolution to the problem of trivial pursuits by returning to God: "Why are you cast down O my soul, and why are you disquieted within me? Hope in God; for I shall again praise him, my help and my God" (Psalm 42:5).

Our longing for God sometimes comes out of some depression like the one which diverted the psalmist from his longing for God. Some problem got in the way of worship. He got trapped in his own thoughts of despair. Then, recovering his vision, he saw the disquiet for what it was — a distraction from the longing of his heart for his Creator. Sometimes it takes an extreme experience to get us back to our Maker.

Our longing for God sometimes is uncovered in an emergency. A friend of mine, after a near-death experience in an auto accident, wrote a song about the nearness of God, even in times of danger:

A Prayer Away

God is just a prayer away
He knows what's happening — night and day
He knows our heart and he knows our mind
Because he's so gracious, so loving and kind.

He gave us his only begotten Son
Who died on a cross, but a victory was won
He died as our Saviour, and set all men free
And all were set free — even sinners like me.

Now there are those who have eyes, but still can't see
And those who have ears, but still can't hear
The story of God and his son Jesus Christ
Who walked on this earth before paying the price.

There is God the Father and God the Son
God the Spirit — three in One
To be BORN AGAIN we must invite all three
To dwell in our hearts 'til eternity!

God is just a prayer away
He knows what's happening night and day
He knows our hearts and he knows our mind
Because he's so gracious, so loving and kind.
— by Orlain Ambrose

Our longing appears to be a longing for relief from some problem. Often we need to find ourselves in some suffering before we realize that we have drifted from God again. We find ourselves dislocated, only to find our real location is with God. We seek relief. God gives us more. He gives us himself. God is our relief.

Our longing appears to be a longing for purpose. We drift into purposes which only distract us from our true purpose to enjoy and glorify God forever. We seek meaning. God gives us more. God gives us himself. God is our purpose and our meaning.

Our longing seems to be a longing for return to our home. We try this or that in the far off country, only to remember that we are away from our home. We seek home. God gives us more. God gives us himself. God is our home.

Recently while on vacation, my wife Joyce and I once again visited our friend Lois in Monterey Bay, California. Her home is on the eighteenth fairway of one of the world's most beautiful golf courses, the course I had played some years earlier. A deer passed by, just ten feet from Lois' house. I thought, "What a great privilege it is to be made in the image of God and to be able to return to our Creator through the powerful presence of his Son."

I remembered the words of Saint Augustine: "Restless are our hearts, O Lord, until they rest in Thee." That return to God is made possible through Jesus Christ and his death on the cross. I also remembered the words of Saint Patrick from "The Deer's Cry." As I looked at the deer, I prayed, "Christ be with me, Christ within me...."

As I looked at the deer just ten feet away, the song "As the Deer" based on Psalm 42 came to mind:

As the deer panteth for the water,
so my soul longeth after Thee.
You alone are my heart's desire,
and I long to worship Thee.[19]

When I thought about God, the beautiful Pebble Beach Golf Course seemed like just one more trivial pursuit.

Questions For Meditation
Or Group Discussion

1. Have you ever seen an animal or something in nature which suddenly turned your attention to God? Describe it.

2. What are some of the trivial pursuits you see people longing after today?

3. Briefly describe the spiritual journey of Saint Patrick.

Chapter 8

God Is Our
Refuge And Strength

---

*God is our refuge and strength, a very present help in
trouble.* — Psalm 46:1, NRSV

* * *

What comes to your mind when I say the word "trouble"? Problems at home with a spouse or children? Problems with a mother or father? Problems at work? Moral problems? Relationship problems? Money problems? Health problems? When we hear the word "trouble," we probably think of some problems which are not easily resolved.

The ancient psalmist who wrote Psalm 46 faced problems too. We are not sure what they were, but we know that when he thought about trouble, he thought about God who is like a strong fortress. That is why he wrote: "God is our refuge and strength, a very present help in trouble."

Martin Luther put this psalm to music. His song is sometimes called the battle hymn of the Reformation. The title is, "A Mighty Fortress Is Our God." When Luther thought of troubles, he also thought of God, our refuge and strength.

The danger is that when troubles come, they can capture us and enslave us, if we do not turn to God. Psalm 46:1 is a great memory verse for this week. Repeat it daily. It will help you with your troubles, whatever they are.

Turning From Troubles
E. Stanley Jones, a Methodist missionary and evangelist, once made this observation about turning from troubles: "Whatever gets

your attention, gets you!" That is the theme which runs through his autobiography, *The Song of Ascents*. It is not what happens to us in life which matters, but what gets our attention and how we react to what happens which determines how we come out. Jones was able to ascend and live above his troubles because God got his attention.

When troubles come, some people turn to money as a possible solution. This is especially true if the troubles are money troubles. Getting some additional money may help, but at best this resolution is temporary and, at worst, money as a problem solver becomes money, the false god which does not deliver what it promises.

I know a man named Tom whose mother died when he was an eleven-year-old boy. Tom could not or did not express his grief. He turned against God, not knowing who else to blame. The family was not Christian. The family was poor. Tom decided very early in life that he would become a millionaire before he was thirty years old. He went after money compulsively. He got what he wanted. When I met Tom, he was a thirty-year-old millionaire. He was also one of the most miserable people I have ever met. Money had become his god. It enslaved him. He had plenty of things, more than he needed, but things got his attention and made him a slave. Troubles triumphed.

The question of life is not "Will troubles come?" They come to all of us. The question is: "Will troubles triumph or will we triumph over troubles?" Money is not the resolution for troubles. When we turn to money as a refuge and strength, money becomes a new problem.

When troubles come, some people turn to power as a way out. Often powerful people have had some serious problems of inferiority and turn to power to right the situation. This looks like an attractive solution to the trouble of feeling put down and being taken advantage of, but gaining a position of power does not resolve the feeling of being powerless. When we turn to power as a refuge and strength, power becomes a new problem. When power gets our attention, power corrupts and as they say, absolute power corrupts absolutely.

When troubles come, some people turn to education. This may be a good solution if the troubles come from a lack of information. This is often the case in both health problems and theological problems. The right information in the medical field has saved lives and reduced pain. We should be glad that we live in this time when so many new scientific discoveries have been made to extend life in quantity and quality, but health problems are not only a matter of improved medical research. Some health problems call for a better understanding of theology.

For example, we all need to have a theological understanding of God, church, and ourselves when health troubles come to our lives. Often people, like Tom mentioned earlier, blame God for their troubles or feel that they are being punished for something they have done wrong. Theological education is important because it deals with getting a higher perspective on what happens to us. But even here, we are not at the secret of the psalmist.

A theologian went to heaven and was told to get into the long line of people waiting to be ushered into the presence of God or get into the short line for theologians. "Where does the short line go?" he asked. "It leads to a lecture hall where an angel will explain the answers to all theological questions." He got into the long line. Theological education helps, but we need more than education about God.

It is not just answers we need. We need God. If answers get our attention, then we can get caught up in answers. We may want answers, but we need God.

When troubles come, some people turn to family and friends. These are the people who stay with us in times of troubles. A little girl was suffering a serious illness. Her father who was a Christian said, "God will help you get through this." She thought for a moment and then replied, "Right now I need a God with a skin on." Don't we all?

That is what Luther means when he says that we are called to be "little Christs" to one another. But friends and family have their limits when it comes to resolving our troubles. They are imperfect. They also die. If friends and family get our attention instead of God, we still end up in despair.

Some years ago I said to a dying cancer patient, "It is sure a good thing that you have friends and family at a time like this." "Yes," she replied with a twinkle in her eye, "but you have forgotten something." "What is that?" I asked. "Faith," she replied. "You forgot about faith. Family and friends are important, but faith is absolutely essential."

"God is our refuge and strength, a very present help in trouble," the psalmist wrote.

Turning In Faith To God In Times Of Trouble

The story of Job in the Bible is helpful when it comes to considering how to triumph over troubles. Like the psalmist, Job turned his attention to God, but before he did, he listened to his friends and family. Not all friends and family are "little Christs" to people in trouble.

Job suffered physically, psychologically, and spiritually. His troubles were many. His friends, representing the bad theology of his time and thinking that Job's troubles were a punishment for his evil deeds, advised him to confess the terrible sins he had committed. Only then would his troubles end. His wife told him to crawl up on a dung heap, curse God, and die. With friends and family like that, who needs enemies?

After many struggles, Job moved his attention from self-pity to bad advice from friends to worse advice from his wife, to faith in the living God who was a very present help. "God is our refuge and strength." When troubles come, we must turn back to God.

E. Stanley Jones described the turn to God like this:

> If you focus on sins and glance at God, your sins will get you. If you focus on resentments and glance at God, resentments will get you. If you focus on your troubles and glance at God, your troubles will get you. But if you glance at your troubles and focus on God, God will get you.

Whatever gets your attention, gets you. When troubles come, give your attention to God.

That is the secret of the psalmist — not just turning *from* troubles, but turning *to* God. When God has your attention, God has you. That is what brings resolution to troubles. That's how to triumph over troubles.

Only God can lift us above the circumstances. If you do not pay attention to God at the center, if you marginalize him, if you just glance at him and do not trust him, you will remain under your troubled circumstances.

Saint Paul learned the secret of the psalmist and expressed it magnificently in Romans 8:31-34.

> *What then are we to say about these things (troubles)? If God is for us, who is against us? He who did not withhold his own Son, but gave him up for all of us, will he not with him also give us everything else: Who will bring any charge against God's elect? It is God who justifies. Who is to condemn? It is Christ Jesus, who died, yes, who was raised, who is at the right hand of God, who indeed intercedes for us. Who will separate us from the love of Christ?*

In verses 35-37 Saint Paul lists troubles he himself has experienced, troubles which almost made him a victim until he rose above the circumstances. We pick up the secret of the psalmist in verse 35:

> *Who will separate us from the love of Christ? Will hardship, or distress, or persecution, or famine, or nakedness, or peril or sword? As it is written, "For your sake we are being killed all day long; we are accounted as sheep to be slaughtered."*
>
> *No, in all these things we are more than conquerors through him who loved us.*

What does "more than conquerors" mean? A conqueror is one who, by might, overcomes an enemy with power. What is more than a conqueror? One who overwhelms another with sacrifice and love. In both cases, the one conquered submits, but in the one case the submission is forced, causing resentment and a desire for revenge. In the other case, the submission is made gladly to a superior who has sacrificed for us and loved us, the result of which is responsive love. That is what Christ has done. He overwhelmed us with his death on the cross.

What is "more than a conqueror"? A victor. Christ is the victor on the cross. He makes us victors by what he has done for us. Rising to the burning white heat of the glory of God as shown in the cross of Christ, Saint Paul reaches for the meaning of being a victor, instead of a victim, by giving our focused attention to God in times of trouble.

> *No, in all these things (troubles) we are more than conquerors through him who loved us. For I am convinced that neither death, nor life, nor angels, nor rulers, nor things present, nor things to come, nor powers, nor height, nor depth, nor anything else in all creation, will be able to separate us from the love of God in Christ Jesus our Lord.* — Romans 8:37-39

Our troubles remain, even compound, but they don't triumph over us. In Christ, we are not victims; we are more than conquerors. We are victors through God who loves us.

The next time you think about your troubles, think about this Bible verse: "God is our refuge and strength, a very present help in trouble."

Questions For Meditation
Or Group Discussion

1. List three kinds of troubles people have.

    1)

    2)

    3)

2. Have you ever met anyone like Tom (described in this chapter)? If so, describe him/her.

3. Why did the theologian choose the longer line in heaven?

4. What is more than a conqueror?

Chapter 9

Clean Hearts
And Renewed Spirits

Create in me a clean heart, O God, and put a new and
right spirit within me. — Psalm 51:10, NRSV

* * *

Why not memorize Psalm 51:10 and repeat it each day this week? This verse shows us how to deal with the enemies in our own hearts and minds. Often, we are our own worse enemy. Unclean hearts and wrong spirits can bog us down in the mire of soul despair. That is why we need this verse about clean hearts and renewed spirits.

There is an extreme potential in each of us for both evil and good. Both sides of human nature are revealed in this great psalm verse. David, the psalmist, had fallen into the pit of despair because he followed his lower nature. He also rose to great heights of spirituality when he followed his higher nature. As a human being made in the image of God, David returned to the Lord and was restored.

Unclean Hearts And Wrong Spirits
An anonymous poet described our two natures like this:

Two Natures
Within this earthly temple there's a crowd
There is one of us that's humble; one that's proud.
There is one that is sorry for his sins
One that unrepentant, sits and grins.
From much corroding care I would be free,
If I could just discover which is me.

They are both me. The struggle within is a struggle between these two forces. We see these forces at work in David, the psalmist. We see them in ourselves as well.

We were created "a little lower than the angels," but sometimes we act like little devils. There are two sides to each of us. The question is not "Are we bad or good?" We are both. The question is "Which one of these forces will win out?"

Another anonymous poet described the plight of being caught between the forces of evil and good like this:

> *There is so much bad in the best of us*
> *And so much good in the worst of us*
> *That it hardly behooves any of us*
> *To talk about the rest of us.*

We will look at the both sides of our human nature as we examine Psalm 51. "Create in me a clean heart, O God, and put a new and right spirit within me" (Psalm 51:10).

"Create in me a clean heart, O God ..." the psalmist writes. What does it mean that God gives us clean hearts? The first thing we must do is to acknowledge that our hearts are unclean.

The heart, with its pumping of blood to all parts of the body, is basic for life. Heart trouble means trouble in all parts of the body. When the veins get all clogged up, the whole body suffers. Someone recently told me, "I just had triple bypass surgery. Now I feel like a new man."

It is the clogging up of our spiritual side which the ancient psalmist has in mind when he pleads with God to give him a clean heart. Psalm 51 lists three ways that our spiritual hearts get clogged up.

First, *transgressions* clog up the spiritual heart. Transgression is a matter of conscious rebellion. "Have mercy on me, O God, according to your steadfast love; according to your abundant mercy blot out my transgressions," the psalmist writes (51:1).

The origin of this psalm is revealing. David, the King of Israel, committed adultery with a beautiful woman named Bathsheba. He saw her bathing on her balcony one day and he lusted after her. He was a man of power. He knew that it was wrong to lust after another man's wife, but he proceeded with the affair, driven by his will to have this woman, whatever the cost. When Bathsheba got pregnant, David tried to cover his transgression by sending her husband Uriah, one of David's warriors, to the front lines. David's rebellious attitude cost Uriah his life.

The prophet Nathan appeared before David one day and asked the pointed question, "How would you judge a man who was wealthy and powerful who stole from a man who was weak and needy?" David, the King, who frequently had to make judgments about people's behavior, said that the man should be punished severely. Nathan, the prophet, responded, "You are the man."

Psalm 51 is David's response to having his transgression revealed. "Blot out my transgressions ..." (51:1), he wrote. "Create in me a clean heart, O God" (51:10). You can feel the passion and the drama of repentance and forgiveness in the Psalm. Transgressions separated David from his source of power. He was revived, restored, and reinstated.

We too transgress. We know something is wrong, yet we proceed with it, not realizing the consequences of our actions. Is it possible to be restored? Yes, but we, like David, must repent. When we do, God casts our sins from us.

As Psalm 103:12 says, "As far as the east is from the west, so far he removes our transgressions from us."

Unclean hearts are filled with transgressions, willful disobedience. Unclean hearts are also filled with iniquities.

Second, *iniquities* clog up the spiritual heart. David wrote, "Wash me thoroughly from my iniquity ..." (Psalm 51:2).

Iniquity means error, or straying from God's ways, as David strayed when he followed his lust instead of his God. Right from the beginning of time, we see the tendency to stray from God's ways. The story of Adam and Eve not only illustrates how we go in erroneous ways, it also shows how we try to cover up for what we do, refusing to acknowledge that we have done wrong.

God said to Adam, "You may eat of all of the trees of this garden, except this one tree." The one thing forbidden is the one thing desired most of all. Eve tempts Adam to eat of the forbidden fruit. Adam relents and does what he knows is against God's will, making a major error of judgment. Then he compounds the error by trying to cover it up and blaming Eve.

God finds Adam hiding behind a bush. "What have you done?" God asks. "It wasn't me. Eve made me do it." When Eve is confronted, she blames the snake. "He made me do it," she says. We have here the classic game of "P.T.B.," "Passing the buck."

This game of "P.T.B." is played in homes and offices, between children and their parents and between friends. It results in compounding the original error by refusing to acknowledge that we have done wrong. Iniquity compounded by iniquity clogs things up in human relationships. Refusing to take responsibility for the error of our ways means that we do not have clean hearts.

When Nathan said to David, "Thou art the man," David repented. Many today, following the example of Adam, say, "Not me. Someone else made me do it. It was the fault of my parents and the way they raised me. I am not guilty. Someone else is to blame." David, setting a pattern of health said, "Wash me thoroughly from my iniquity and cleanse me from my sin" (51:2).

The third way this psalm describes an unclean heart is *sin*. "Cleanse me from my sin," David wrote (Psalm 51:2). Sin is our self-centered tendency to miss the mark. It means that we cannot see beyond our own little world. In theology, the German word *umvelt* is used to describe this condition. It means that I don't see the big picture because I am all caught up in my little world.

A psychiatrist wrote in his journal about a patient named Edith, that there was little hope of helping her. Here is what he said: "Edith is bound on the east and west, the north and the south by Edith."

Edith is not the only one who has this problem. We all have it! Psalm 51 shows us the way out of the dilemma of being bound on every side by ourselves. There is a war going on in every one of us — a war between evil and good. The way out of the dilemma called sin is repentance, turning from self to God.

One part of me says, "I did not do it. Don't blame me." That is the part which is called original sin. By nature I am sinful and self-centered. That is what Psalm 51:5 means when it says, "In sin did my mother conceive me." If that tendency is not overcome, I come out a loser and find only misery and death.

But there is hope. God also placed a bit of himself in me. That part says, "Confess your sin and return to God." David chose the better part and said, "Create in me a clean heart, O God...." Thus David's spirit was renewed. We, too, can have renewed spirits by choosing the better part.

Clean Hearts And Renewed Spirits

David said, "Create in me a clean heart, O God, and put a new and right spirit within me" (Psalm 51:10). How can I have a new and right spirit? By repentance and return.

Repentance means turning back to God when we have gone astray. Repentance results in revival of our flagging spirits, restoration of the joy that has been missing, and reinstatement of our relationship with our God. I especially like the Brandt paraphrase of Psalm 51:10-12.

> Revive my flagging spirit, O God
> Restore to me the joy and assurance of a right
> relationship with You.
> Reinstate me in Your purposes, and help me to
> avoid the snares and pitfalls along the way.[20]

Consider the three words, *revive, restore* and *reinstate*, and behold what happens when God gives clean hearts and renewed spirits as we turn back to him with repentance.

Let me describe this journey back to God in story form. It is one thing to hear the truth of God, another to feel the truth of it. Sometimes we feel it better when we hear it in story form. This is the true story of Jay Dull.

In 1961, Jay Dull murdered a taxicab driver in Muncie, Indiana. Jay and his friend, Walter, had taken the taxicab driver out into the country to rob him. When the cab driver lunged for the gun, it went off and shot him. Jay and his friend, Walt, jumped in the cab and drove back to town, leaving the cabdriver in the country where he froze to death. It is plain to see that the lower natures of Jay Dull and Walt were at work in the robbery and the murder. It got worse.

At his trial, Jay was asked the question, "Aren't you sorry for what you did?" The belligerent, arrogant criminal responded, "Hell, no. Given the same circumstances, I'd do it again." Jay Dull was convicted of murder and assigned to the electric chair. He ordered his last meal, had his head and leg shaved, and came within twelve hours of being electrocuted. A stay of execution from the governor of Indiana, in response to the pleas from Jay's mother, saved his life physically, but from a spiritual point of view, Jay seemed like a hopeless case.

I met Jay in the county jail in Muncie in 1962. One of his relatives was a member of Holy Trinity Church where I was the pastor. "Will you go see him?" his relative asked. Reluctantly I went, but frankly I thought that a pastoral call was useless. When Jay told me that he had turned his life over to Christ, I thought at first that it was what is called "jail-house religion," saying that you are sorry in order to avoid the consequences of evil actions. After visiting Jay over a period of several months, I became convinced that Jay was sincere in his repentance.

It was my pleasure to see this murderer turn his life over to the Savior. "I deserve this punishment," Jay said, "but I need to be made right with God." I heard Jay's confession, instructed him in the Christian faith, and confirmed him in the Muncie jail in 1963. Jay's higher nature responded to the gospel that Christ had died for him and for his forgiveness.

Most of us have not gone to the extremes of adultery like King David or murder like Jay Dull, but we have the same potential for evil that they had. We also have the same potential to turn back to God, because God has placed a bit of himself in all of us. It is called "the image of God." There is something in us onto which God latches. In theology this is called the *anknügfunktspunkt*, the buttoning-on point. God placed something of himself in each of us so that, like a button and a buttonhole, we fit together with God when we return to him. When that happens, God revives us, restores us, and reinstates us.

First, God revives us. All of us get tired and discouraged. It is very encouraging to hear that God revives our flagging spirits.

Our spirits can be revived. Jesus says, "Come unto me all you who labor and are heavy laden and I will give you rest" (Matthew 11:28). When burdened down with problems and sins, we can be revived. That is why we have a Savior who loves us.

Second, our spirits can be restored. Jeremiah, the prophet, wrote, "Return O faithless children. I will heal your faithlessness" (Jeremiah 3:22). Let me paraphrase the message of God's prophet: "If you return, I will restore you" (Jeremiah 4:1). We can be restored because we have a Savior who has mercy on us.

Third, we can be reinstated to the status of God's children, seeking to do God's will and following his purposes. We can be reinstated because we have a Savior who died for us.

After being away from God all of her life, a new Christian recently told me, "This church has made all the difference in the world for my life. I am a new person. I was judgmental and resentful. Life looks very different now. For the first time in my life, I feel that I am not alone. God is on my side. God was there all along, I just did not see it before."

It is my privilege as a pastor to see the worst and the best in people. Pastors see both the selfish and greedy side when people reveal their sins in confession or when relatives fight with one another over who will inherit what at the time of a death. We also see the best in some people as they turn back to God and have their spirits renewed. That is one of the reasons I like the anonymous poem about the two sides of human nature so much.

> There is so much bad in the best of us
> And so much good in the worse of us
> That it hardly behooves any of us
> To talk about the rest of us.

Questions For Meditation
Or Group Discussion

1. Describe the two-sided nature of human beings.

2. Transgressions are:

3. Iniquities are:

4. Sin is:

5. What revives us, restores us, and reinstates us?

Chapter 10

It Is High Time

Shout with joy to God, all the earth! Sing glory to his name; make his praise glorious! — Psalm 66:1-2

* * *

There are two parts to the Christian faith — the vertical and the horizontal. Here we focus on the vertical, our relationship with God through worship.

Psalm 66 is a psalm about worship. It is also a psalm of worship. Leslie Brandt, in *Psalms Now*, paraphrases Psalm 66:1-2 like this: "It is high time we start making happy noises about God...." That means *high* time and high *time* for worship and adoration.

High time is different than low time. *High* time means adoration of the Almighty. Most people today are caught in the web of low time, living as if this is a one-story universe, as if there is nothing on the second story. Many live today as if there is nothing but this earth — no heaven, no God, no afterlife.

It Is *High* Time For Worship And Adoration

Worship is the ultimate resolution of the ultimate human problem — loneliness — and yet many neglect it, making religion only a matter of trying to be good.

A clergyman took his seat on a plane next to a rather sober-looking gentleman who, when he saw the collar on the minister said, "My friend, I see that you are a clergyman. I would like to make it clear from the outset that I do not wish to talk about theology. I am an astronomer, and my faith is summarized in these words, 'Do to others what you would have them do to you.'" The scientist was a humanist, seeing religion only in terms of how you treat others, with no adoration of the Almighty through corporate worship.

The clergyman replied, "I am glad that you have found a simple and satisfying religious concept. I happen to have found a simple and satisfying concept of astronomy: 'Twinkle, twinkle, little star.' " It was a long plane ride.

The Christian religion consists of two parts, one horizontal, one vertical. The horizontal part represents how we treat our neighbors. The vertical has to do with adoration of the Almighty in worship. One without the other is heresy. Together they form a cross, the central symbol of our faith. Adoration of the Almighty through worship is the biblical corrective for a distorted humanism.

Those of us who worship together regularly each Sunday are more apt to remember adoration of the Almighty — high praise, as a central ingredient of our faith — but we too need to be reminded about the importance of a focus on God.

Peter, once he saw Jesus walking on the water coming toward the boat where he sat, got up and started to go to the Lord, walking on water. Suddenly the wind came up and the waves started to roll. Peter took his eye off of the Lord and began to sink.

The Christian faith is centered in keeping your eye on God. That is what adoration is all about. Regular worship helps us to focus on God in the storms of life. Worship and support from the worshiping community keep us from sinking when the storms of life come.

It is *high* time! Time for worship of God, keeping our eyes focused on God.

Why have Christians gathered for worship each Sunday for the last 2,000 years? Because they know the secret of the second story of this universe. Jesus came from the "second story" to show us that there is more, much more, than just this earth, as we live out our days. "I came to give you life," he said, "life in abundance." The abundant life means learning to fall on one's knees and adore the Almighty. It is *high* time!

The psalmist wrote: "Praise God with shouts of joy, all people! Sing to the glory of his name; offer him glorious praise! Say to God, 'How wonderful are the things you do!' " (Psalm 66:1-2, TEV).

That is adoration. Without adoration, our prayer life and worship life are shallow. Adoration of the Almighty God is a missing ingredient for most people in modern times. They live as if there is nothing more than one dimension — this world — to living. When death comes, there is no resource to tap.

It is *high* time to worship God with adoration and praise. The psalmist reminds us, "Praise God with shouts of joy, all people!" That is a timely reminder for all of us.

About adoration Saint Augustine said, "Lord, you made us for yourself and our hearts are restless until they rest in you." Adoration is resting in God.

Teilhard de Chardin said, "To adore means to lose oneself in the unfathomable, to plunge into the inexhaustible, to find peace in the incorruptible ... to offer oneself to the fire ... and to give one's deepest to that whose depth has no end."[21] Adoration is losing oneself.

The Bible says, "You shall love the Lord your God, with all your heart, with all your soul, with all your mind, and with all your strength." Adoration means loving God.

David Adam, a writer about Celtic spirituality and the vicar at the Lindesphar Christian community just off the coast of Scotland, says that adoration is simply reciprocal love.[22] Adoration is resting in God, losing oneself in God, and loving God.

A peasant woman at the altar of her church was interrupted in her prayers by her pastor one day. "I'm sorry to interrupt your prayers," the pastor said, "but I have a question for you. I've noticed that you are at church each Sunday and at communion each time it is offered. I have also noticed that you often come to church and spend many hours on your knees praying. I am working on a sermon on adoration. I just wondered if you could define it for me."

"That's easy," she replied. "Adoration just means, 'God looks at me and I look back at him.' "

Sometimes it takes a crisis or some other shift from normal life for us to have a heightened awareness of the Presence of God, to realize as the peasant woman said, that God is looking at us and we are looking at him.

David Adam in his book, *The Open Gate*, puts it like this:

> *... New vistas often come before us at a point of crisis in our lives, when we are suddenly bereaved, or made redundant or when we are having what the world calls a breakdown. Often we become more aware because we have become dislocated, just as we are more aware of a limb that is dislocated. If we face the unfamiliar it may open all sorts of gates for us (especially the gate called glory).*

On Monday, July 29, 1996, while in Durham, England, for a study of the Celtic Christian, a new awareness of God and adoration of the Almighty came upon me. I had been feeling very dislocated — I knew no one. No one knew me. I had just arrived in Durham for my study of "Celtic Spirituality And Modern Mission." I went to a 7:30 a.m. communion service at the 903-year-old cathedral, which was built by Celtic monks 400 years before Columbus discovered America.

The morning was gray and misty. The cathedral was dark. As I looked up, I saw beams of light intersect the great beams of the old church. I touched one of the old giant pillars and remembered the dedication of the monks and builders who had constructed this immense cathedral to the glory of God. I smelled something. At first I thought that it was just the dampness, but there was something else. I followed the smell. It was the smell of altar candles at one of the side altars where an Anglican priest was preparing communion for us. I felt the Presence of God in this old place of worship. When I knelt on a pillow on the old stone floor I thought of Psalm 66:1-2: "Shout with joy to God, all the earth! Sing glory to his name; make his praise glorious!"

It was *high* time.

It Is *High Time* For Praise

Isn't it *high time* that we recognize that "God looks at me and I look at him"? Isn't it *high time* that we personally apply the words of the psalmist?

Praise God with shouts of joy, all people! Sing to the glory of his name; offer him glorious praise! Say to God, "How wonderful are the things you do!"

Isn't it *high time* that we learn about adoration from the peasant woman who said, "He looks at me and I look back at him"? Isn't it *high time* that we recognize what Saint Augustine meant when he said, "Restless are our hearts until they find rest in you"? That's adoration! Augustine had a Christian mother named Monica who prayed for him often, but he went astray. He got caught in the web of a false religion, one of his own making. He got a girl pregnant and had an illegitimate son. Then one day under the preaching and guidance of a pastor (Ambrose), he turned to Christ and gave him his life. He came to worship and adore the one, true God. That's why he could say, "Lord, you made us for yourself and our hearts are restless until they rest in you!"

Isn't it *high time* that we rediscover the ultimate resolution of our ultimate problem of loneliness? Isn't it *high time* that we turn back to our Creator with praise and adoration? Isn't it *high time* that we recognize what God is doing for us? The psalmist urges a high time of return to worship as a central ingredient for a life with meaning and adoration.

Adoration. Some people who do not worship on a regular basis try to use God in emergencies. Not having worshiped God, they don't know him and his ways of using the Christian community for support in times of need. When bad things happen, people with a strong faith grounded in regular worship often just barely make it through. Those outside the worshiping community are beaten down further by troubles.

Adoration. Isn't it *high time* that we recognize what the Bible means when it says that we are to "love the Lord your God, with all of your heart, with all of your soul, with all of your mind and with all of your strength"? Isn't it time, *high time*, that we get away from the false gods of this world and get back to adoration of the Almighty?

Adoration. Isn't it *high time* for reciprocal love? In Christ, God loved us first. Isn't it *high time* to return that love?

101

On my trip to Ireland, England, and Europe, to study the early forms of Christianity, I listened to many unchurched people tell me that their religion consisted of trying to be moral and good to other people. "What do you do for a living?" I asked a man named Peter from Australia. "I'm a government worker." We talked further. "What is your religion?" I asked after we had talked about other topics sipping wine in Florence, Italy. "My religion? Oh, I'm a Lutheran," he said, "but I don't go to church anymore. I believe that since I am a good man, God will send me to heaven when I die. By the way, what do you do for a living?" "I'm a Lutheran pastor," I said. Then I paused, wanting to say something helpful to help Peter think again about worship, the sacraments and the Word of God, all of which point us toward adoration.

"If we could go to heaven by being good," I said, "then why did Christ die on the cross for us?" That is the ultimate question we all need to answer. Isn't it *high time* to look at Christ on the cross so that we respond in the words of the Christmas carol, "O come let us adore him, Christ the Lord"?

Peter had no answer to that question. He was living as if we lived in a one-story universe. He changed the subject, but I hope he thought about the question later.

Adoration is the heart of our religion. Adoration of God is the fulfillment of our destiny. We look at Christ on the cross and he looks back at us.

Adoration means looking at God, resting in God, losing oneself in God, and loving God who first loved us. Isn't it *high time* to get back to adoration? Isn't it *high time* to look back at God who is looking at us? Isn't it *high time* we start "making happy noises about God ... and shout his praises"?

Questions For Meditation
Or Group Discussion

1. Have you ever had a "high time" of worship at a church camp, on a retreat, or at a Sunday worship service? Describe it.

2. Adoration means:

3. The Australian Peter said, "I don't need to go to church. I'm a good man." What's the problem with that philosophy?

Chapter 11

That The Next
Generation Might Know

---

*He (God) decreed statutes for Jacob and established
the law in Israel, which he commanded our forefathers
to teach their children,* **so the next generation would
know them,** *even the children yet to be born, and they
in turn would tell their children. Then they would put
their trust in God and would not forget his deeds but
would keep his commands.* — Psalm 78:5-7

* * *

Psalm 78:5-7 describes passing the faith on to the next genera-
tion and to generations yet to be born. The statutes and laws for
Israel and for the new Israel, the Christian Church, are eternal.
One generation after another must learn them and keep them to
avoid the errors of the past. But how shall people learn the truths of
God? Someone has to teach them. Someone has to lead them.

In Bible times the responsibility to teach and lead often fell to
the elders. The elders were the ones who were wise by virtue of
their age and experience. The elders were the leaders of Israel and
the early Christian Church. They taught the children Bible stories.
They led the way by example.

In May we celebrate Mother's Day. Each May we also celebrate Children's Day at King of Glory Lutheran Church in Fountain Valley, California. In June we celebrate Father's Day. Why not
celebrate a new holiday, Elders' Day, at which we remember and
celebrate all who teach and lead in God's church? You don't have
to be old to be an elder in God's Church. You just need to teach
and/or lead.

On Elders' Sunday we give thanks for all who have taught a children's or adult Sunday School class, all who serve or have served on the church council or in some other leadership capacity in the church. We also celebrate any Christian parent who has taught his/her children. On Elders' Sunday I applaud Christians for teaching and leading, so that the next generations may know God and his ways.

Elders Teach!

In Bible times the elders taught, not because they were retired and had more time than mom and dad, but because elderly people, due to their experiences, were considered the wise ones. The most precious truths of the faith had to be passed on to the children and the children's children. Who better than the wise ones, the elderly of the town, tribe, or family to tell the stories of faith and family?

In Bible days, the elderly were not "put out to pasture." They were revered. Everyone respected their opinions. They were considered wise. The elders attended the college of "hard knocks" and passed their experience on to others. Their experience made them wise. They were the ones who shared the experience of faith through Bible stories, and passed the great truths of religion on to the next generations. They housed the treasures of the years in their hearts. They passed these treasures on to the young through teaching.

What did they teach? They taught the laws of God. They taught the stories of God. They taught the stories of the Bible. They taught the mighty deeds of God.

Psalm 71 is about the elders and their ministry as teachers. Psalm 71:5-9 says:

> *For you have been my hope, O Sovereign LORD, my confidence since my youth. From birth I have relied on you; you brought me forth from my mother's womb. I will ever praise you. I have become like a portent (prophetic indication or significance) to many, but you are my strong refuge. My mouth is filled with your praise, declaring your splendor all day long. Do not cast me away when I am old; do not forsake me when my strength is gone.*

106

Psalm 71:17-18 continues the theme of the elders as valuable teachers of the mighty deeds of God.

> *Since my youth, O God, you have taught me, and to this day I declare your marvelous deeds. Even when I am old and gray, do not forsake me, O God, till I declare your power to the next generation, your might to all who are to come.*

What did they teach? They taught right doctrine, as Titus 1:9 says:

> *He (an elder) must hold firmly to the trustworthy message as it has been taught, so that he can encourage others by sound doctrine and refute those who oppose it.*

Declaring the marvelous deeds of God and right doctrines of God is the way of teaching the next generations about faith in God. The elders were mostly lay people. Pastors, the name given to teaching and preaching elders later in the history of the Church, taught too. Lay people and pastors worked together to bring the faith to the next generations.

Listen to the way Saint Peter describes the teaching ministry of both lay people and pastors: "To the elders among you, I appeal as a fellow elder ..." (1 Peter 5:1).

Saint Paul appointed elders to teach the people of God in all of the churches he started. Lay people and pastors worked together to pass the faith on to future generations. That's what we need today — a partnership of lay people and pastors working together that the next generations might know God and his ways.

A preacher in the early Church named Apollos had to be corrected by two of the lay elders appointed by Saint Paul. Apollos was mixed up in his doctrine about Baptism. Priscilla and Aquila had to help Apollos distinguish between the baptism of John the Baptist and the Baptism of Jesus.

Meanwhile a Jew named Apollos, a native of Alexandria, came to Ephesus. He was a learned man, with a thorough knowledge of the Scriptures. He had been instructed in the way of the Lord, and he spoke with great fervor and taught about Jesus accurately, though he knew only the baptism of John. He began to speak boldly in the synagogue. When Priscilla and Aquila heard him, they invited him to their home and explained to him the way of God more adequately. When Apollos wanted to go to Achaia, the brothers encouraged him and wrote to the disciples there to welcome him. On arriving, he was a great help to those who by grace had believed. For he vigorously refuted the Jews in public debate, proving from the Scriptures that Jesus was the Christ.

— Acts 18:24-28

Lay people and preachers are teaching elders in partnership so that the next generations might know. A pastor was telling one of his council members about his suffering, and the problems he was having with some church members. "Under these circumstances," he said, "I don't know if I can go on." The council member was an old-timer who had been through many troubles. With a twinkle in his eye, he smiled and said, "Under these circumstances? I thought you said in your sermon last Sunday that we are to live above our circumstances, not under them." That council member was a teaching elder, like Priscilla and Aquila.

Christian elders are people who rise above their circumstances which would crush others. They pass on the faith that overcomes to the next generation, because they themselves are overcomers. Overcomers not only have experience which qualifies them as teachers, but also they generally have a good sense of humor.

An elderly Christian woman not only had endurance in suffering; she also had a wonderful sense of humor about what was happening. She wrote:

The Joys Of Aging
I have become quite a frivolous old gal. I'm seeing five gentlemen every day. As soon as I awake, Will Power

helps me out of bed. When he leaves I go see John.
Then Charley Horse comes along and when he is here,
he gets a lot of my attention. When he leaves, Arthur
Ritis shows up and stays the rest of the day. He doesn't
like to stay in one place very long so he takes me from
joint to joint. After such a busy day, I'm really tired and
ready to go to bed with Ben Gay. What a day!

That is what helps the elders to teach the young about God —
a mature faith sprinkled with humor which means that they don't
take themselves too seriously.

Another elderly Christian, who was hard of hearing, attended
a funeral and heard the pastor say: "Hearing is the last thing to go
with those who are dying." At the reception following the funeral,
she had a twinkle in her eye as she told me: "You said that hearing
is the last thing to go for the dying, didn't you?" "Yes," I replied.
"Well," she said, "I can hardly hear anything, so I guess I won't
see you next Sunday."

Humor like that, combined with a faith which has gotten someone through the trials and tribulations of life, results in the faith
being passed on to future generations.

Elders teach. They also lead.

Elders Lead

The Westminster Bible Dictionary of the Bible defines the word
"elder" in terms of leadership in church and society:

> *An official who, so far as can be judged, had by virtue*
> *of his right as first-born, succeeded to the headship of*
> *a father's house, of a tribal family, or of the tribe itself.*
> *Ordinarily, only men of mature age came into these*
> *positions. The title designates high officials generally*
> *in Genesis 50:7. They exercised authority over the*
> *people (Deuteronomy 27:1). A body of 70 elders as-*
> *sisted Moses in the government of the Israelites. Each*
> *town had its elders, who were probably the heads of*
> *the several family connections in the place and who*
> *administered its civil and religious affairs.*

> In the churches founded by the apostles, elder or
> presbyter and bishop were interchangeable designations
> (cf. Acts 20:17 with v. 28, R.V... The former had pri-
> mary reference to the dignity of the office, the latter to
> its duties. The distinction between elder (or presbyter)
> and bishop, as 2 separate orders of ministers, dates
> from the 2nd century. The origin of the office of elder is
> not recorded, but elders existed practically from the
> beginning. In A.D. 44 they already existed in the church
> at Jerusalem (Acts 11:30). Paul on his First Mission-
> ary Journey appointed elders in every church.
>
> The office of elder in the Christian Church was
> evidently suggested by the office of elder among the
> Jews, and was invested with similar authority. Elders
> were associated with the apostles in the government of
> the Church (Acts 15:2, 4, 6, 22, 23; 16:4; cf. 21:18).
> They were the bishops or overseers of the local churches
> (ch. 20:17, 28; Titus 1:5), having the spiritual care of
> the congregation, exercising rule and giving instruc-
> tion, and ordaining to office (1 Timothy 4:14).[23]

The elders in the early Church were leaders who cared for the
people in the congregations they served.

1 Peter 5:1-4 describes the work of leadership among the Christian elders in terms of shepherding:

> To the elders among you, I appeal as a fellow elder, a
> witness of Christ's sufferings and one who also will
> share in the glory to be revealed: Be shepherds of God's
> flock that is under your care, serving as overseers —
> not because you must, but because you are willing, as
> God wants you to be; not greedy for money, but eager
> to serve; not lording it over those entrusted to you, but
> being examples to the flock. And when the Chief Shep-
> herd appears, you will receive the crown of glory that
> will never fade away.

The elders in ancient Israel and in the early Christian Church
were the teachers of Bible stories and leaders by example. They
saw what needed to be done and did it.

At a recent conference on leadership which I attended, one of the speakers explained leadership in terms of action. Leith Anderson said:

> *Most leaders in the twenty-first century will not be well-known personalities. They will be the people in the shadows, both lay leaders and pastors, who see what needs to be done and do it. They will not be perfect. Often, they will be flawed to a fault, just like the leaders in the Bible. It isn't that they have special traits of leadership, but that they do what needs to be done. They just will do what needs to be done, whatever that is.*
>
> *Some leaders are exuberant, some quiet; some dynamic, some not very dynamic but stable; some very spiritual, some not so spiritual. The one thing they will do is to do what needs to be done.*
>
> *Recently, I heard the Larry King show on television. He was interviewing one of the boys involved in the Springfield, Oregon school tragedy, where 24 teens were shot by a student who went out of control. The shooter was tackled by a wrestler who was wounded but moved forward to stop the shooter anyway. The boy being interviewed was Jacob Ryder, the boy who dove on the gun that fell within reach when the wrestler downed the shooter. Larry King asked him, "Why did you go for the gun when you might have run?" "I don't know," he said.*
>
> *"That," said Anderson, "is what most leaders say. They go for the gun; they don't run. Leaders say they don't know why they lead. They just do it." Anderson concluded, "Leaders may not always know why they do what they do, but they do what needs to be done, whatever it is."*

Leith Anderson then added two stories about leaders. The first story was about a young pianist who played a marvelous concert in London. The audience applauded loudly. "Go back on stage," said the stage manager. "No," said the young pianist. Then the audience rose and gave the pianist a standing ovation. Still the pianist refused to go back on stage. "There's a gray-haired man in the balcony who is not standing," he said. "That's only one man," said the stage manager. "He's my teacher," said the young pianist.

The second story is about Saint Stephen, an elder in the early Church.

> *When they heard this, they were furious and gnashed their teeth at him. But Stephen, full of the Holy Spirit, looked up to heaven and saw the glory of God, and **Jesus standing at the right hand of God**. "Look," he said, "I see heaven open and the Son of Man standing at the right hand of God." At this they covered their ears and, yelling at the top of their voices, they all rushed at him, dragged him out of the city and began to stone him. Meanwhile, the witnesses laid their clothes at the feet of a young man named Saul. While they were stoning him, Stephen prayed, "Lord Jesus, receive my spirit." Then he fell on his knees and cried out, "Lord, do not hold this sin against them." When he had said this, he fell asleep. And Saul was there, giving approval to his death. On that day a great persecution broke out against the church at Jerusalem, and all except the apostles were scattered throughout Judea and Samaria.*
> — Acts 7:54—8:1

Note that Stephen, the elder, saw Jesus standing for him. May Jesus stand and applaud you for what you are doing as you rise above your circumstances with faith and humor as a teaching and leading elder in God's Church.

Questions For Meditation
Or Group Discussion

1. What qualities are needed by Christian teachers and leaders?

2. What was Apollos' problem?

3. How does humor help a teacher or preacher?

4. Name some people you believe God is applauding as teaching and leading elders.

Chapter 12

The Bread Of Life

They forgot what he had done, the wonders he had shown them. He did miracles in the sight of their fathers in the land of Egypt, in the region of Zoan. He divided the sea and led them through; he made the water stand firm like a wall. He guided them with the cloud by day and with light from the fire all night. He split the rocks in the desert and gave them water as abundant as the seas; he brought streams out of a rocky crag and made water flow down like rivers. But they continued to sin against him, rebelling in the desert against the Most High. They willfully put God to the test by demanding the food they craved. They spoke against God, saying, "Can God spread a table in the desert? When he struck the rock, water gushed out, and streams flowed abundantly. But can he also give us food? Can he supply meat for his people?" When the LORD heard them, he was very angry; his fire broke out against Jacob, and his wrath rose against Israel, for they did not believe in God or trust in his deliverance. Yet he gave a command to the skies above and opened the doors of the heavens; he rained down manna for the people to eat, he gave them the grain of heaven. Men ate the bread of angels; he sent them all the food they could eat. He let loose the east wind from the heavens and led forth the south wind by his power. He rained meat down on them like dust, flying birds like sand on the seashore. He made them come down inside their camp, all around their tents. They ate till they had more than enough, for he had given them what they craved.

— Psalm 78:11-29

*   *   *

Do you ever get discouraged? Do the difficulties of life ever get you down? Do you ever feel distraught or distracted from God by the circumstances of life? Of course you do. Life is difficult. Bad things happen to everyone, even to good people. The Word from God in Psalm 78 is addressed to this kind of situation. It is a Word about renewal by remembering and celebrating the Presence of God. The Bible is God's manual for survival on this small planet. Psalm 78 is about remembering and celebrating God's gift of the bread of life for nourishment to overcome the discouragements and distractions of life. In Psalm 78, we are told that the people of God moving through the wilderness forgot that God had given them bread from heaven.

We are called today to remember that God has given us the bread of life and to celebrate that God continues to give it to us daily and abundantly.

Remember What God Has Done

Psalm 78:11 says: "They forgot what he had done...." This verse reminds us that all believers can get distracted from a focus on the bread of God with which we are nourished for renewal. In the pressures of life, we can forget to remember the mighty deeds of God. To forget to remember means that while we can recall something and repeat it, we do not re-member it, literally give it members again, make it live today. That's what happened to the Hebrew people according to Psalm 78:11. They forgot to re-member the mighty deeds of God. Frequently the Hebrew people forgot to remember their holy history in the exodus.

Have you heard the real reason why the Israelites wandered in the wilderness for forty years? Even then, men would not stop for directions. Seeking God's directions is the secret of the pilgrims of God wandering in the wilderness of life.

God led the people of Israel out of the bondage of Egypt. He divided the Red Sea and allowed the Hebrews to go through. He led the people of God with a pillar of cloud by day and a pillar of fire by night. He split the rock and gave them water when they were thirsty. He sent quail when they protested that they had no meat to eat. In addition, God sent manna from heaven as the people wandered in the wilderness for forty years.

In their wanderings, God gave them food for the journey. They got discouraged, but received the encouragement to go on through the gifts of God. For the Jews, the reference to manna became a way to remember what God did to get them through discouraging times.

When you get discouraged, the psalmist says, remember the manna from heaven. Manna means "What is it?" That is what the Hebrews said when they found the bread-like stuff on the ground. Moses told them it was bread from heaven which would nourish them for the journey through the wilderness, but he warned, "You must gather it fresh each morning." As you can guess, fearful that one morning God would not keep his word, the Hebrews tried to store up the manna. The stored-up manna was rotten. When you get discouraged, don't forget that the manna must be gathered each new day, the psalmist says.

To gather manna fresh each morning means that we do not take our faith for granted, that we do not think that yesterday's knowledge will get us through today. We must put the faith of our fathers into play today. We cannot depend on the fact that we believed in the past to get us through the wilderness today. God's manna must be fresh each morning. Faith must be renewed each day.

Our human malady is that we often forget to remember God's directions. It is not that the content of our holy history is lost; it is just that we don't call it forth today. That is what the word "remember" means — "to call forth from memory." Psalm 78 is a reminder to call up the content of what God has done. God gave us the bread of life in the past. God will deliver the bread of life in the present. God answered the needs of his people when they called on him daily in the past. He answers those needs today as well, when we call upon him daily. God not only answers our needs, he answers them daily. He not only answers our needs daily; he answers those needs abundantly.

As the psalmist says, "They ate till they had more than enough, for he had given them what they craved" (Psalm 78:29). We are called to remember what God has done. In Hebrew, to remember means more than to recall. To remember means more than just learning the lessons of history. To remember means to call forth something in the past in such a way that it becomes present reality.

That is one of the reasons Jesus taught us to pray in the Lord's Prayer, "Give us this day our *daily* bread." God gave the Hebrews food, daily and abundantly. Because they were afraid that God would not keep his word daily and abundantly, they depended on themselves and what they could store up instead of on God's promises. Jesus taught us to give thanks for food daily to help us remember what the Hebrews forgot and avoid the trouble they had.

Since daily bread comes from God, we should thank God for our food at each meal. The bread of life is the food we receive from God each day for sustenance. A new Christian from China visited America and made this amazing remark: "I was shocked to see that there were so few Christians here. We ate out in several restaurants and we never saw anyone bow their heads in prayer before a meal." To celebrate what God gives daily not only means that we should thank God for each meal, whether we are at home or in a restaurant. It also means that we should thank God regularly for Holy Communion.

In the institution of the Lord's Supper, Jesus said, "Do this to *remember* me." He meant that as we receive the Sacrament, he will come rushing forward from the past and meet us in the holy elements. In Holy Communion we do more than recall an event from the past. Jesus meets us in the bread of life. That is why we speak of remembering and celebrating Holy Communion.

Celebrating What God Is Doing

Are you discouraged about something or someone? If so, celebrate what God has done and what God is doing to renew you with the bread of life today.

In John 6:31 Jesus says, "Our fathers ate the manna in the desert; as it is written: He gave them bread from heaven to eat ... I am the bread of life. He who comes to me will never go hungry." We are called upon not only to remember what God has done, but to celebrate what God is doing. Celebration is about present-tense religion, religion which renews and gives life today. God did not say, "My name is I was." God did not say, "My name is I will be." God said, "My name is I am." Jesus said, "I am the bread of life." Jesus spoke of himself as the bread of life, the fulfillment of the gift of manna from heaven. We not only remember what Jesus did; we receive what Jesus is doing today. That is present-tense religion to help us overcome discouragement and start again. Our daughter Mary Cousler wrote this poem about starting over again.

Start All Over Again
Life is strange. It ebbs and flows;
*   it rises and it falls.*
When things get tough, it's common to stop;
*   it happens to one and all.*

But strange as it is, one thing is sure:
*   it's up to us every one*
To pick ourselves up, dust ourselves off
*   and start all over again.*

Life is a choice, to win or to lose,
*   to lead or follow a crowd.*
"Never give up, give in, give out!"
*   true leaders shout out loud.*

It's easy to hear the words of a jeer
*   in place of an uplifting thought,*
But deep in the soul the knowledge unfolds
*   of good things yet unwrought.*

"You're down, you're out, there is no hope!"
*   the critics jeer and call.*
You feel you've lost, you're done, you're through,
*   you're backed up against the wall.*

But deep inside you realize
*   that it's all up to you.*
It's in your mind, the dream, the goal;
*   it's yours to make come true.*

So when the dark times come to you,
with all their grief and pain,
Pray and sing; you can beat this thing
and start all over again.

— Mary Lavin Cousler

Daily, God gives us his Son, the bread of life, to start over again. What is God doing? God feeds us daily with the bread of life, nurturing and encouraging us to start again once more, urging us and feeding us today with his Presence. We are called to thank God daily for all he does in the present.

The bread of God is more than physical food. The bread of God is also the eternal food which comes through the Word and the Sacraments where the eternal bread comes to us today.

An alternate translation of the Lord's Prayer reads: "Give us tomorrow's bread today." What is tomorrow's bread? That is the bread which comes from the kingdom of God, the bread which strengthens us for the work of the kingdom of God, the manna from heaven which gives us a foretaste of the feast to come in the kingdom of God. Tomorrow's bread comes to us in the Holy Sacrament.

One of the words on which our English word "daily" in the Lord's Prayer is based is *epiousion*. That means food for today. Another ancient word on which our word "daily" is based is *machar*, which means tomorrow's food today. It may very well be that what Jesus prayed and urged us to seek is tomorrow's bread today. Tomorrow's bread is the bread or nourishment of the kingdom of God which is coming. Tomorrow's bread is the bread from the kingdom which is coming that nourishes us today.

Jesus said, "I am the bread of life." That means that in the bread and wine of Holy Communion, Jesus is near. That means that in the Lord's Supper, Jesus is here. "Do this to remember me," Jesus said. When we re-member him, Jesus comes rushing forward as our contemporary. He does not leave us desolate (John 14:18). He is near. He is here.

As the pastor says, "The body and blood of Christ given and shed for you," remember and celebrate the powerful and personal Presence of God in your life. At the Lord's Supper you are given more than enough, more than you craved to start over again.

Questions For Meditation
Or Group Discussion

1. What brings discouragement to people's lives?

2. How can remembering help?

3. How can celebrating help?

Chapter 13

From Attractive Distractions To Singing God's Steadfast Love

I will sing of your steadfast love, O LORD, forever;
with my mouth I will proclaim your faithfulness to all
generations. I declare that your steadfast love is estab-
lished forever; your faithfulness is as firm as the
heavens. — Psalm 89:1-2, NRSV

* * *

Let me invite you to memorize Psalm 89:1, "I will sing of your steadfast love, O LORD, forever," and repeat it daily this week. Memorizing and repeating a verse like this can help you respond to God's steadfast love in your lifestyle and greatly enrich your spiritual life.

The leader of worship in the Temple sang, "I will sing of your steadfast love, O LORD, forever" (Psalm 89:1). The congregation responded, "With my mouth I will proclaim your faithfulness to all generations." The leader sang, "I declare that your steadfast love is established forever." The people responded, "Your faithfulness is as firm as the heavens." To sing means more than to make music. It means to respond to the steadfast love of the Lord with word and deed.

First, let us look at steadfast love in the Bible. Then we will look for steadfast love in our lives today.

Steadfast Love In The Old Testament

The steadfast love of God is the theme of this Psalm. In Hebrew the word for steadfast love is *chesed. Chesed* is one of the most important words in the Old Testament. It is used 148 times in the Old Testament. While it is not necessary for us to know this or any other Hebrew word to get into heaven, there is no chance for us to enter heaven without the benefits of *chesed*. *Chesed* means that God is steadfast, merciful and faithful, even when we are not. *Chesed* means that God is dependable, even when we are not. *Chesed* means that God does not forget us even if we forget him. *Chesed* means that God always shows loving-kindness toward his children who are not always loving or kind.

Chesed is not only the theme of this psalm; it is used about 100 times in other Psalms to portray the heart of God. *Chesed* is celebrated frequently in the prayer book of the Bible which we call Psalms. In addition, God's steadfast love is the theme of one of the greatest love stories in the Bible — the story of Hosea and Gomer. Sometimes people say that the Old Testament contains only law and the New Testament only gospel. Actually, both the New Testament and the Old Testament have law and gospel. The story of Hosea and his wife, Gomer, is pure gospel, pointing beyond itself to the gospel of our Lord Jesus Christ

Hosea, a prophet of God, married Gomer, a woman with a shady past in sexual matters. He was morally upright, she promiscuous. He was faithful like God; she faithless like Israel. The marriage itself symbolized the way in which God continued to love his people, even when they did not deserve his love. Two of the children born of this marriage were named "Not My People" and "Not Pitied" (No Mercy), names Hosea chose because they were symbolic of the way the people should be treated by God because of their lack of faithfulness.

Gomer grew restless in the marriage relationship. Perhaps shame, because of her earlier sexual immorality, caught up with her. Perhaps she committed adultery while married. Whatever the reason, one day Gomer deserted her family. She turned to prostitution. She sold herself to men of lust for a price.

Some years later, the day came, as it comes to all of us, when Gomer had to face the consequences of her immorality. She was old and unattractive physically. Once a beauty, Gomer was now an overweight, ugly old woman. Her sins had caught up to her. Her sexual attractiveness was lost. She was being sold as a slave in

Jerusalem. As the auctioneer tried to sell her, the crowd laughed as the auctioneer mocked her. In terms of our money, the auctioneer might have said something like this: "Who wants an old prostitute? Who will offer a few dollars for this worthless old woman? Maybe she can be bought for a few pennies."

Everyone laughed. No one bid. The mockery continued for what seemed like hours. Can you feel the humiliation and shame that this woman felt? She had a low opinion of herself as a young girl. Why else would she be promiscuous? That low self-image dropped considerably when she deserted her loving husband and children. Why else would she become a prostitute? Now no one would pay even a few pennies to purchase her. Feel the shame.

Hosea, who was in Jerusalem at the time, happened to pass by. Seeing his wife, he was humiliated for her. Being moved with compassion as he beheld her in ultimate shame and mockery, he cried out, "I will buy her back. She is mine. I will pay."

That's what God is like. He buys us back when we have no value, when we are utterly worthless, hopeless, and lost. It is God's nature to show *chesed* — faithfulness, loving-kindness, and steadfast love — when we are unworthy.

No wonder the psalmist, knowing the heart of God, declares, "I will sing of your steadfast love, O Lord, forever" (Psalm 89:1). In the New Testament we come face-to-face with this steadfast love of God in the person of Jesus.

Steadfast Love In The New Testament

In case you are wondering what ever happened to Hosea's children, "Not Pitied" ("No Mercy") and "Not My People," the New Testament answers that question.

> ... *You are a chosen race, a royal priesthood, a holy nation, God's own people, in order that you may proclaim the mighty acts of Him who called you out of darkness into His marvelous light. Once you were **not a people**, but now you are God's people; once you had **not received mercy**, but now you have received mercy.*
> — 1 Peter 2:9-10, NRSV

The New Testament shows us that the love of God in the person of Jesus Christ reverses the judgment of God. Jesus died on the cross for us, demonstrating God's steadfast love for sinners.

I think you can see why I have asked you to memorize and daily repeat this Bible verse: "I will sing of Your steadfast love, O Lord, forever." This verse is the summation of our faith in the God of steadfast love. In the New Testament, the Greek word which carries the message of steadfast love is *agápe*, God's love for sinners. *Agápe* is used in many favorite New Testament verses.

In John 3:16, we read about *agápe*: God so loved the world that he gave his only begotten Son, that whosoever believes in him should not perish but have everlasting life.

1 Corinthians 13 tells us about the steadfast love of God in Christ called *agápe*.

> *If I speak in the tongues of men and of angels, but have not love, I am only a resounding gong or a clanging cymbal. If I have the gift of prophecy and can fathom all mysteries and all knowledge, and if I have a faith that can move mountains, but have not love, I am nothing. If I give all I possess to the poor and surrender my body to the flames, but have not love, I gain nothing. Love is patient, love is kind. It does not envy, it does not boast, it is not proud. It is not rude, it is not self-seeking, it is not easily angered, it keeps no record of wrongs. Love does not delight in evil but rejoices with the truth. It always protects, always trusts, always hopes, always perseveres. Love never fails. But where there are prophecies, they will cease; where there are tongues, they will be stilled; where there is knowledge, it will pass away. For we know in part and we prophesy in part, but when perfection comes, the imperfect disappears. When I was a child, I talked like a child, I thought like a child, I reasoned like a child. When I became a man, I put childish ways behind me. Now we see but a poor reflection as in a mirror; then we shall see face to face. Now I know in part; then I shall know fully, even as I am fully known. And now these three*

*remain: faith, hope and love. But the greatest of these
is love.*

1 John 4:8 says, "God is *agápe*." In 1 John 4:10 we hear the
good news that while we are yet sinners, God continues in his *agápe*:
"In this is love, not that we loved God but that he loved us and sent
his Son to be the expiation for our sins."

We are looking right into the heart of God. God is faithful,
even when we are faithless. Faithfulness can make all the difference
in the world. This is what *agápe* means. God paid the price for our
sins on the cross. God has accomplished what only God can do.
But we must appropriate what has been accomplished by
repentance. The cross of Christ is the best demonstration of how
far God will go with his steadfast love to bring us back. Jesus'
death on the cross cries out, "I'll buy them. They are mine." What
happens to sinners who desert the loving God? They are bought
back by the blood of the cross. This is the good news of Calvary.
God pays the price for our sins. He has accomplished your
salvation.

The New Testament not only tells us what God's love has accomplished; it also tells us that some people reject that love. Some
fail to appropriate what has been accomplished. God has given his
love to everyone. Everyone receives what has been given, but some
people never personally accept what they receive. God makes out
the check. Some people do not turn the check over and personally
endorse it.

Some people get distracted by the attractive distractions of the
world. Others get distracted by good things instead of focusing on
the best thing as we see in Luke 10:38-42, the story of Martha who
worked hard in the kitchen, but neglected to listen to Jesus as he
explained God's love to Mary, Martha's sister.

> *Now as they went on their way, he entered a certain
> village, where a woman named Martha welcomed him
> into her home. She had a sister named Mary, who sat
> at the Lord's feet and listened to what he was saying.
> But Martha was distracted by her many tasks; so she
> came to him and asked, "Lord, do you not care that my*

sister has left me to do all the work by myself? Tell her then to help me." But the Lord answered her, *"Martha, Martha, you are worried and distracted by many things; there is need of only one thing. Mary has chosen the better part, which will not be taken away from her."*
— Luke 10:38-42, NRSV

We are all easily distracted from the love of God. One thing is needed: listening to the story of God's love and responding by passing it on. Work is a good thing, but it can be an attractive distraction, keeping us from the best thing. The best thing, the one thing needful, is hearing about God's steadfast love and passing it on. Jesus said to Martha, "You are worried and distracted by many things ..." (Luke 10:41, NRSV). Many people today are distracted from the one thing needful, not only by work, but by money, possessions, sex, sports, entertainment, and sins. One thing is needful: to appropriate personally the steadfast love of God which has been accomplished through Jesus' death on the cross. To appropriate what God has accomplished is called response.

God's Steadfast Love In Our Lives

The worship leader said, "I will sing of your steadfast love, O Lord, forever" (Psalm 89:1a). The people responded, "With my mouth I will proclaim your faithfulness to all generations" (Psalm 89:1b). Jesus demonstrated the steadfast love by this death on the cross. How shall we respond?

Recently I met an 82-year-old man named John. As we got acquainted, he shared that his wife had Parkinson's Disease, a debilitating illness which causes a major change in personality. "She is very negative and angry all the time," John said. "She has been kicked out of four nursing homes. I'm a Christian, but there are days when I wonder how I can continue on like this." There were tears in his eyes as he spoke. John went on, "Every day I arise and say, 'This is a day the Lord has made. Let us rejoice and be glad in it.'" That's what I call bringing forth fruit with faithfulness and persistence! That's what I call "singing of the steadfast love of God!" That's what I call response!

A Christian woman felt called to respond to God by ministering to the people in an asylum for the mentally ill. She visited regularly, although the response to her calls was minimal. She was fascinated by a woman named Anne, who would not even answer the simplest of questions. Anne did not respond to anyone.

"It is no use doing anything for that one," everyone told her. "She is so far gone that no one can help her." The woman visitor persisted in trying to reach this strange patient, but to no avail. Finally, she decided to bring the woman some brownies. The doctor said, "You can try it, but it won't do any good. She is a lost soul."

The next time she visited Anne, the visitor noticed that one brownie was gone. It was an opening. Little by little over a long period of time, Anne opened up. Anne began to respond to the steadfast love of God shown by the visitor. Finally, the day came that Anne was released. Soon thereafter she was hired to work with a blind and deaf girl named Helen. Everyone said that Helen was dumb.

The rest of the story of Anne Sullivan is history. Persistently, Anne worked with Helen, overcoming obstacles which seemed impossible to overcome. The day came when all the efforts finally bore fruit. "W-A-T-E-R," Anne spelled out in the hand of little Helen at the water pump. "It is water." Helen began to learn that things have names. She was smarter than anyone dreamed. The day came when Helen Keller went on a lecture tour and astounded the world with her wisdom. Helen sang out the praise of God by her witness because Anne Sullivan had done the same. The unnamed woman who would not give up at the asylum with the girl named Anne, sang out her response with persistent love and care which changed countless lives through Helen Keller.

A New York businessman who had recently become a Christian, decided that he wasn't being loving enough. He hadn't followed God's lead of loving-kindness as he now wanted to do. In church on Sunday and in his morning prayers on Monday, he promised to be a more loving Christian, "even if it kills me."

He rushed to the train station to catch a train to Boston. He was in a hurry. He was running late. The conductor cried out "All aboard!" He started running. His suitcase hit something. He looked down and saw a small boy who had been carrying a large jigsaw puzzle. Now dozens of puzzle pieces littered the platform.

The boy started crying. The train started moving. Just as the man was getting ready to make a run for it, he remembered his promise to God. So he set his bags down, patted the boy on the head, smiled and said, "I'll pick it up for you." While he gathered all the pieces of the puzzle and put them in the box, the train pulled away. The little boy was watching him intently. When he had finished putting the lid back on the box and handed it to the boy, the boy looked up with a kind of wonder and said, "Mister, are you Jesus?"[24]

The businessman missed his train, but he did not miss the message of God about loving-kindness and steadfast love. God's steadfast love in Jesus Christ comes to us. Then it is supposed to go through us to others.

Questions For Meditation
Or Group Discussion

1. As a child, did anyone show loving-kindness to you? How?

2. Give an illustration of *agápe* from the New Testament.

3. How would you describe Helen Keller's discovery?

Chapter 14

When The World Oppresses You

LORD, thou hast been our dwelling place in all generations. Before the mountains were brought forth, or ever thou hadst formed the earth and the world, from everlasting to everlasting thou art God. Thou turnest man back to the dust, and sayest, "Turn back, O children of men!" For a thousand years in thy sight are but as yesterday when it is past, or as a watch in the night. Thou dost sweep men away; they are like a dream, like grass which is renewed in the morning: in the morning it flourishes and is renewed; in the evening it fades and withers. For we are consumed by thy anger; by thy wrath we are overwhelmed. Thou hast set our iniquities before thee, our secret sins in the light of thy countenance. For all our days pass away under thy wrath, our years come to an end like a sigh. The years of our life are threescore and ten, or even by reason of strength fourscore; yet their span is but toil and trouble; they are soon gone, and we fly away. Who considers the power of thy anger, and thy wrath according to the fear of thee? So teach us to number our days that we may get a heart of wisdom. — Psalms 90:1-12, RSV

* * *

"Burdens, burdens, burdens. All I have are burdens," the woman said as she slouched down on the counselor's couch. She was oppressed by the world in which she lived.

Sometimes it feels like everything goes wrong, not just for a day, but for a long, long time. Troubles come in bunches and seem to last forever. Problems seem insurmountable. It feels like something or someone out there is against us. It feels like the world is oppressing us.

The oppressive troubles may take the form of sickness, monetary problems, family difficulties, troubles with a spouse, troubles with a child, troubles with a parent, or troubles with a friend.

In this study of the Psalms, we are looking at the prayer book of the Bible. The Psalms help us to get a perspective on what is happening in life by looking beyond this world. We not only say the Psalms; we pray them. Today we turn for help to Psalm 90.

The memory verse for the week before us is Psalm 90:1: "LORD, you have been our dwelling place in all generations." If you repeat that verse daily, you will be in touch with a dynamic way to deal with the oppressive forces of life. This Bible verse puts us in touch with the God who is from everlasting to everlasting (Psalm 90:2).

O God, Our Help In Ages Past

When the world oppresses you, it is a good time to turn to Psalm 90 and God, who is our dwelling place. The hymn, "O God, Our Help in Ages Past," based on Psalm 90, puts it this way:

> *O God, our help in ages past,*
> *Our hope for years to come,*
> *Our shelter in the stormy blast,*
> *And our eternal home.*
> — Isaac Watts

When oppressive forces are at work in our lives, we can go back to our eternal home. God is our help in ages past, our shelter from the stormy blast of life's oppressive forces. The psalmist urges believers to remember that their eternal home is with God. He urges us to look back on the God who existed before the world began — before the mountains, earth, and sea were formed. He urges us to get in touch with eternity in the past. How do you deal with the oppressive forces of the world? By remembering that God is your eternal home, and that he sends help in time of trouble. What does it mean that God is our eternal home?

First, God as our eternal home means that we must go back to God as our foundation. The rains will come down. The winds will blow and beat against your house. Christians and non-Christians alike must face the forces of oppression in life. But if you build your house on the rock, it will stand.

In the Sermon on the Mount Jesus addressed this situation of overcoming the oppressions of the world. He said, "Build your house on a rock."

> *"Therefore everyone who hears these words of mine and puts them into practice is like a wise man who built his house on the rock. The rain came down, the streams rose, and the winds blew and beat against that house; yet it did not fall, because it had its foundation on the rock. But everyone who hears these words of mine and does not put them into practice is like a foolish man who built his house on sand. The rain came down, the streams rose, and the winds blew and beat against that house, and it fell with a great crash." When Jesus had finished saying these things, the crowds were amazed at his teaching, because he taught as one who had authority, and not as their teachers of the law.*
> — Matthew 7:24-29

Second, having an eternal home means that we need to go back to our roots. When oppressive forces come, turn back to the roots of your faith, God, as our dwelling place. You must have roots in the eternal if you are going to cope with the oppressive forces of the world.

There is a story about Grandpa who had a toothache, but Grandpa would not cooperate with the dentist. "Open up," the dentist said, but Grandpa shook his head, "No." "I can't work on your toothache if you don't open up," the dentist said, but Grandpa refused. "Come back tomorrow," the dentist said. The next day the same thing happened. Following Grandpa's second failure to open his mouth, the dentist told his nurse that when Grandpa returned the next day, if he refused to open up, she should stick him in the bottom with a long needle. He would then open up, and the dentist could pull the bad tooth.

The same thing happened on the third day. The dentist nodded to the nurse who jabbed Grandpa, who opened up, allowing the dentist to pull the bad tooth. "Now that wasn't so bad, was it, Grandpa?" the dentist inquired. "No," replied Grandpa, "but the roots were sure deep."

Deep roots — that's what we need for help to face the oppressive forces around us, roots which go down deep. Having an eternal home with God means having roots.

Third, to have God as our dwelling place means that God is our help when oppressive forces come. At such times God will deliver. You can depend on him.

> There was a great flood in the Midwest. A deeply religious man, who loved his home, refused to leave when the police came by and warned him, "The flood is rising. You will have to evacuate. Get in the car." "No," he said, "I'm praying, and I know that God will save me."
>
> When the waters rose to window level, a boat of friends and neighbors came by. "Get in," they said. "No," said the man. "God will save me. I'm praying to Him."
>
> When the waters rose to roof level, the man climbed to the very peak of his house. A helicopter came by. "Grab the rope and get on board," the pilot shouted. "No," said the man, "God will save me."
>
> As you might expect, the waters continued to rise and the man drowned. When he got to heaven, he complained to God, "Why didn't You hear my prayers? You've always answered my prayers in the past; why didn't You save me this time?" God responded, "I tried, but you just weren't listening. I sent you a police car, a boat and a helicopter, but you would not get on board."

For help with living and hope to overcome death, we must turn to God and watch for the messengers he sends. God is "Our help in ages past, and our hope for years to come," the hymn writer says.

O God, Our Hope For Years To Come

When the psalmist thought about the future and growing old, he wrote, "So teach us to count our days that we may get a heart of wisdom" (Psalm 90:12).

As he looked to the future, as he got older and approached death, the psalmist saw that our only hope is with God, our hope for years to come. This is the one essential. Many things are important, but God is essential. Consider three important ways to plan for getting old.

First, we want to grow old with *security*. Financial security is important, but as a hope for the future, all financial security fails. A modern insurance company has been running an ad on television lately. The theme is "Be your own rock." They are urging financial security by investing with them. It may sound good to build enough financial security that you are your own rock, but it just doesn't work. Financial security doesn't solve all the problems of life.

It is important to plan for retirement with secure pension and investment plans, but all of these plans eventually come crashing down. You can build your house on the sandy foundation of financial security, but when the rains of suffering come and the wind of death blows, that house will come crashing down. To stake your hopes on financial security is foolish. God, teach us to count our days and apply our hearts to wisdom and turn to the essential hope we have in you. God is our security.

Second, we want to grow old with *family* and friends. Family and friends are important as we grow old, but as an ultimate hope for the future, all people fail us. It is helpful to have a secure family — spouse, children, and grandchildren. But when the winds and storms of life come, your house will come crumbling down if it is built on the foundations of family.

A woman who was dying of cancer was surrounded by good people who really cared for her. "You are blessed to have so many friends and such a good family," I said. "Yes," she replied, "but you have forgotten something. I know friends and family are important, but faith is essential." That woman applied her heart to wisdom and built her house on the rock called faith in God.

As an ultimate hope for the future, all human systems and relationships fail us. Some systems are better than others. Leading a good life in selfless service of other people is better than leading a life of selfishness; but in the end, even the best people die. When you are faced with getting older and facing death, there is only one foundation which will last. That foundation is God.

Third, we want to grow old *gracefully* and with *longevity*.

A Roman Catholic nun wrote this poem about growing old gracefully:

Seventeenth-Century Nun's Prayer

Lord, Thou knowest better than I know myself that I am growing old. Keep me from the fatal habit of thinking I must say something on every subject and on every occasion.

Release me from craving to straighten out everybody's affairs.

Make me thoughtful, but not moody; helpful, but not bossy. With my vast store of wisdom, it seems a pity not to use it all. But Thou knowest, Lord, that I want a few friends at the end.

Keep my mind free from the recital of endless details. Give me wings to get to the point.

Seal my lips on my aches and pains. They are increasing — and love of rehearsing them is becoming sweeter as the time goes by.

I dare not ask for grace enough to enjoy the tales of others' pains, but help me to endure them with patience.

I dare not ask for improved memory, but for a growing humility and a lessening cock-suredness when my memory seems to clash with the memories of others. Teach me the glorious lesson that occasionally I may be mistaken.

Keep me reasonably sweet. I do not want to be a saint — some of them are so difficult to live with. But, a sour old person is one of the crowning works of the devil.

Give me the ability to see good things in unexpected
places, and talents in unexpected people. And give me,
Lord, the grace to tell them so.
  Amen.

We want to grow old gracefully. We also want to live long, productive lives. We want *longevity.*

A woman wrote a poem on her eightieth birthday about longevity:

Today, Dear Lord, I'm 80,
  and there is so much I haven't done.
I hope, Dear Lord — just let me live
  until I'm 81.

But then if I haven't finished all I
  want to do,
  would you let me stay awhile,
    until I'm 82?

So many places I want to go ...
  so very much to see ...
  do you think that you could manage
    to make it 83?

The world is changing very fast.
  There is so much in store!
  I would like very much to live
    until 84.

And if by then I'm still alive,
  I'd like to stay until 85.

More planes will be in the air ...
  I'd really like to stick
  and see what happens to the world
    when I'm 86.

I know, Dear Lord, it's much to ask
  (and it must be nice in heaven),

but I would really like to stay
until I'm 87.

I know by then I won't be fast
and sometimes will be late,
but it would be so pleasant
to be around at 88.

I will have seen so many things
and had a wonder time;
I'm sure that I'll be willing
to leave at 89 ...
Maybe!

Longevity is important, but when faced with growing old and when death oppresses you, there is only one essential.

Growing old with security, with family, doing it gracefully and with longevity — yes, these are important, but what is essential? Growing old in the light of eternity! Having God as the rock foundation, our hope for years to come, is the one essential. "Lord you have been our dwelling place for all generations ... Teach us to number our days that we may apply our hearts unto wisdom" (Psalm 90:1,12).

O God, our help in ages past,
Our hope for years to come,
Our shelter from the stormy blast,
And our eternal home.

Questions For Meditation
Or Group Discussion

1. Describe an elderly person who is aging gracefully.

2. What does it mean to have God as our eternal home?

    1)

    2)

    3)

Chapter 15

My Protector

---

*You who live in the shelter of the Most High, who abide
in the shadow of the Almighty, will say to the LORD,
"My refuge and my fortress; my God, in whom I trust."
For he will deliver you from the snare of the fowler and
from the deadly pestilence; he will cover you with his
pinions, and under his wings you will find refuge; his
faithfulness is a shield and buckler. You will not fear
the terror of the night, or the arrow that flies by day, or
the pestilence that stalks in darkness, or the destruction that wastes at noonday. A thousand may fall at your
side, ten thousand at your right hand, but it will not
come near you. You will only look with your eyes and
see the punishment of the wicked. Because you have
made the LORD your refuge, the Most High your dwelling place, no evil shall befall you, no scourge come
near your tent. For he will command his angels con-
cerning you to guard you in all your ways. On their
hands they will bear you up, so that you will not dash
your foot against a stone. You will tread on the lion and
the adder, the young lion and the serpent you will
trample under foot.*   — Psalm 91:1-13, NRSV

*   *   *

The spiritual song, "You Who Dwell In The Shelter Of The
Lord," is based on Psalm 91. The theme of both the psalm and the
song is God's protection of his people.

*You who ... dwell in the shelter of the Lord,
who abide in this shadow for life,
say to the Lord: "My refuge, my rock in whom I trust!"*

143

Snares of the fowler will never capture you,
and famine will bring you no fear;
under God's wings your refuge with faithfulness your
    shield.

For to the angels God's given a command
to guard you in all of your ways;
upon their hands they will bear you up,
lest you dash your foot against a stone.

Chorus:
And he will raise you up on eagle's wings
Bear you on the breath of dawn
Make you to shine like the sun
And hold you in the palm of his hand.

This is a highly personal psalm. In the NRSV translation, the personal pronoun "you" or "yours" is used nineteen times in these thirteen verses. For example,

- "*You* who live in the shelter of the Most High ..." (91:1);
- "He (God) will deliver *you* ..." (91:3);
- "He will cover *you* ..." (91:4);
- "... Under his wings *you* will find refuge ..." (91:5);
- "*You* will not fear the terror of the night ..." (91:5);
- "Because *you* have made the LORD *your* refuge, the MOST HIGH *your* dwelling place, no evil will befall *you* ..." (91:9-10)

This is a psalm not about protection in general, but about personal protection.

This is also a powerful psalm about our powerful God (Psalm 91:1-2 and 4b). This powerful God is called *Shaddai* (Almighty) and *Elyon* (Most High) as an indication that he is stronger than all of our enemies, and all the demons which threaten us.

This is a personal, powerful psalm about protection, which promises that God will cast out seven demons which threaten each of our lives.

God Protects Us By Casting Out Seven Demons

The first demon cast out is the evil warrior who threatens us. Notice the language of warfare.

> *You who live in the shelter of the Most High, who abide in the shadow of the Almighty, will say to the LORD, "My refuge and my fortress; my God, in whom I trust ..." his faithfulness is a shield and buckler* (91:1-2 and 4b).

The evil warrior, the devil, is stronger than we are, but God, our refuge, our fortress, our shield and our buckler, is stronger than the devil. The Bible says that the devil is as strong as a lion: "Your enemy the devil prowls around like a roaring lion looking for someone to devour. Resist him, standing firm in the faith ..." (1 Peter 5:8b-9).

The Bible teaches that God delivers us from the strongest of the demons which threatens us: the devil.

The second demon which is cast out is fear of the fowler or bird hunter: "For he will deliver you from the snare of the fowler" (91:3).

Later in the psalm we will look at the eagle protecting her young. Here we see that the little eaglets might be easily caught by a clever fowler, but not if God protects them. God is stronger and wiser than any evil which tries to hunt us down. There are the traps all throughout our lives; but God will guide us around the traps if we follow him.

The third demon which God casts out of our lives is the night terrors: "You will not fear the terror of the night" (91:5a).

No fear, not even in the valley of shadows described in Psalm 23, will overpower us. No night terrors in the desert of life shall overcome us. Have you ever been in the desert at night? There is nothing darker. Ancient people feared the wild beasts of the deserts and the serpents which emerged in the cool darkness. The dangers and terrors of the night are overcome by the God who sees and acts, even when we are threatened by night terrors.

The fourth demon which God casts out of our lives is the "arrow by day," which Elmer Leslie, an Old Testament scholar, calls sunstroke.[25]

The arrow of day, the sun in the desert, the hottest place on earth, during the hottest hour of the hottest day, cannot bring you down. Why? The sun was created by God. Since God created the sun, God is stronger than the sun. Sunstroke threatened our forefathers who dwelt in the desert, but the arrow that flies by day cannot put you down when God is your protector. God casts out the fear of the sun.

The fifth demon cast out is pestilence or plague. "... or the pestilence that stalks in darkness, or the destruction that wastes at noonday" (91:6).

Pestilence for the ancients took many forms. Plagues still kill by the thousands in underdeveloped countries today, destroying everyone, especially children, like some monster. In America, we may not wrestle with plagues like underdeveloped countries, but we still must deal with monster-like cancer. Many seem to lose that battle. This demon too is put down by our protector, God, who is stronger than death.

The sixth demon is "evil near your tent." "... No evil shall befall you, no scourge come near your tent" (91:10).

In ancient times, desert dwellers lived in tents made of flimsy branches and animal skins. These tents were not very strong. But for those who made the LORD their dwelling place, there was always protection. Your enemies, whatever form they take, would have no trouble getting to you in flimsy man-made tents, but you can dance and sing and dine happily when God is your refuge and strength. Psalm 23 puts it vividly: "Thou preparest a table before me in the presence of my enemies."

The seventh demon is described in terms of the threatening animals of the desert. "You will tread on the lion and the adder, the young lion and the serpent you will trample under foot" (91:13).

You can make a footstool of the king of the beasts, the lion. You can defeat the dreadful cobra when God fights on your side. The imagery is striking. God protects.

146

Best of all, the psalmist uses the image of the eagle in verse 4a of Psalm 91. We are the children of God, the eaglets. God is the mother eagle who protects us and teaches us how to fly.

God Protects Us Like A Mother Eagle Protects Her Young

"He will cover you with his pinions, and under his wings you will find refuge ... " (Psalm 91:4a, NRSV).

Pinions are eagle's wings, the mighty outstretched eight-foot wing span of the mother eagle, under which her eaglets are protected. Israel was protected by these mighty wings. The Church of God is protected by these mighty wings. I am protected by these mighty wings. You are protected by these mighty wings of God. That's what I call protection! The Bible is filled with the imagery of eagles, their strength and protection.

Deuteronomy 32:9-11 describes the strength and protection of God like this:

> *... The LORD'S portion is his people,*
> *Jacob his allotted inheritance.*
> *In a desert land he found him,*
> *in a barren and howling waste.*
> *He shielded him and cared for him;*
> *he guarded him as the apple of his eye,*
> *like an eagle that stirs up its nest*
> *and hovers over its young,*
> *that spreads its wings to catch them*
> *and carries them on its pinions.*

Four protecting actions of the mother eagle are described here:
1) stirring up the nest to help the little ones learn to fly,
2) hovering over them in their first weak efforts at flight,
3) when they begin to fall, swooping under them to save them, and
4) carrying them on eagle wings to safety.

God stirs up our comfortable nests too. He wants us to fly. But he hovers over us, watching our every move. When we begin to fall, he swoops under us and catches us. And he carries us as on eagle's wings to safety. What an image of God's protection of his people! What a picture of God's personal protection for us!

Deuteronomy 33:27 describes God's protection like this: "The eternal God is your refuge, and underneath are the everlasting arms of God."

That's what I call protection and power! But there is more. The eagle has uncanny sight and perspective. From 600 feet up in the air, an eagle can spot an object the size of a dime in six inches of grass. From the distance of five miles' altitude, an eagle can see a small fish jump in a nearby lake.[26] That's what I call powerful perspective!

The eagle eye of God is upon you, watching your every move and having enough perspective from the heights to see things as they really are. God protects us by giving us that kind of perspective of what is happening to us. That is why our strength is renewed.

Isaiah 40:28-31 describes the protection and renewing power of God like this:

> Do you not know?
>> Have you not heard?
> The LORD is the everlasting God,
>> the Creator of the ends of the earth.
> He will not grow tired or weary
>> and his understanding no one can fathom.
> He gives strength to the weary
>> and increases the power of the weak.
> Even youths grow tired and weary,
>> and young men stumble and fall;
> but those who hope in the LORD
>> will renew their strength.
> They will soar on wings like eagles;
>> they will run and not grow weary,
> they will walk and not faint.

Recently while vacationing with our children and grandchildren in Estes Park, Colorado, I sat alone for two hours on the porch of our cottage, overlooking a beautiful valley with snowcapped mountains in the distance and mountains rising on each side of the valley. It was a wonderful time for reflection and meditation on Psalm 91. As I meditated on verse 4a, a bird flew into the valley. It was too far away to see what kind of a bird it was, but in my imagination, I saw the mighty eagle and I thought of this verse: "He will cover you with his pinions, and under his wings you will find refuge" (Psalm 91:4a).

In your mind's eye, picture the scene. Put yourself in the picture as I did. The quiet valley. The snowcapped mountains. The eagle swooping down from the heights, protecting its young, and flying over you, the young bird, as you try out your wings. You falter and wonder what will happen when suddenly out of nowhere, mother eagle comes to your rescue. That is what I call powerful, personal protection. Look. Feel. Hear. Listen.

Listen to the word on the wind: "Underneath are the everlasting arms of God." Feel the power and the care. Hear the word of God: "I will raise you up on eagle's wings ..."

Questions For Meditation
Or Group Discussion

1. As a child, were you ever in a situation where you needed protection? Describe it.

2. The seven demons in Psalm 91 are:

   1)

   2)

   3)

   4)

   5)

   6)

   7)

3. The eagle imagery in Psalm 91:4a and Isaiah 40:28-31 suggests:

Chapter 16

Sing To The Lord A New Song

Sing to the LORD a new song, for he has done marvel-
ous things; his right hand and his holy arm have worked
salvation for him. The LORD has made his salvation
known and revealed his righteousness to the nations.
He has remembered his love and his faithfulness to the
house of Israel; all the ends of the earth have seen the
salvation of our God. Shout for joy to the LORD, all
the earth, burst into jubilant song with music; make
music to the LORD with the harp, with the harp and
the sound of singing, with trumpets and the blast of the
ram's horn — shout for joy before the LORD, the King.
Let the sea resound, and everything in it, the world,
and all who live in it. Let the rivers clap their hands, let
the mountains sing together for joy; let them sing be-
fore the LORD, for he comes to judge the earth. He will
judge the world in righteousness and the peoples with
equity.   — Psalm 98:1-9, RSV

*   *   *

Psalm 98 is a song of enthronement of God as king over all of
Israel. It was a way in which the people of God willingly said, "We
want to start life again under God's dominion." Psalm 98 was a
recognition of God's willingness for us to start again and a resolution on our part to live under God as LORD.

For this recognition and resolution, old songs would not do. In
honor of new beginnings with God, a new song was needed. "It's
beginning again time," the psalmist was saying. "Let's sing praise
to God in a fresh, new way because God is enthroned again as our
LORD." The psalmist looked at nature — the earth, the sea, the

rivers — and saw that God's creation praises him. He looked at musical instruments — harps and trumpets and all instruments — and saw how these can be used to praise God. "Let's add the human voice to the concert," he was saying. Then he thought about salvation, God's victory over evil forces, and he could not contain himself. "Sing to the LORD a new song," he sang, "for he has done marvelous things." To discover God's salvation makes the soul sing out praise to the LORD.

This is the greatest discovery anyone can make in life. The most marvelous thing God has done is to enthrone himself over our lives as LORD, giving us salvation.

Sing To The Lord

Dr. Granger Westberg, lecturing to a group of doctors, nurses, and pastors at the University of Arizona Medical School some years ago, said, "My research has shown that there is one thing which is more important to health than anything else." We, in the audience, were invited to guess. Guesses included a positive attitude, regular check-ups, exercise, a good diet, and good relationships with friends and family. Dr. Westberg said, "My research shows that the most important ingredient in good health is gratitude. Since gratitude is the essence of worship, the best thing we can do for our health is to worship God with songs of gratitude. If you really want to improve your health, join the church choir. Then you can praise God through music twice a week! Do you want to be healthy? The attitude is gratitude."

Singing praise to God is one of the healthiest things we can do. Singing praise can be an expression of gratitude. Gratitude to God is the center of faith. Gratitude is the attitude which brings new life.

The attitude of gratitude means that we turn from self-centeredness to God-centeredness. This turn from self to God as the center is well documented in the psalms. Psalm 98:1 describes this new attitude beautifully as the psalmist looks at the works of the LORD in his life and shouts with joy: "Sing to the LORD a new song, for he has done marvelous things." Other psalms lift up the same theme of a new song which comes from an attitude called gratitude.

> *Psalms 33:3: Sing to him a new song; play skillfully, and shout for joy.*

> *Psalms 40:3: He put a new song in my mouth, a hymn of praise to our God. Many will see and fear and put their trust in the LORD.*

> *Psalms 96:1-3: Sing to the LORD a new song; sing to the LORD, all the earth. Sing to the LORD, praise his name; proclaim his salvation day after day. Declare his glory among the nations, his marvelous deeds among all peoples.*

> *Psalms 144:9: I will sing a new song to you, O God; on the ten-stringed lyre I will make music to you, to the One who gives victory to kings, who delivers his servant David from the deadly sword.*

The attitude of gratitude means that we turn from a turned in view of life to an attitude of stewardship of God's gifts to us. Stewardship means more than how much money we give to the church for God's work. How much money we give and what percentage of our income we give can be a wonderful expression of our attitude of gratitude to God, but stewardship means more. It has to do with using our gifts for God.

Franz Liszt, the famous composer, was once shown an advertisement in a little town newspaper that a certain young piano student was giving a concert. She lied in the advertisement and said that she was a student of the famous composer Franz Liszt. Liszt was going to be near that town in his travels, so he decided to confront the young girl with her lie. He invited her to his residence and asked her why she had said she was his student when in fact that was a lie.

She replied, "I did it to try to get more people to come to my concert. It was a terrible thing to do. I am truly sorry. I promise never to do it again. I apologize from the depths of my heart."

Liszt decided that she was sincere. Yes, he would forgive her, but something more was needed. "Can you do more than apologize?" he asked. "What do you mean? she said meekly. "Can you play?" he asked. "What do you mean?" she asked. "Play the piano for me."

The nervous young girl sat down at the piano and began to play. Liszt made several gentle corrections and then shocked the girl by asking, "Do you mind if I play the last number at your concert?"

You can imagine what happened. She was thrilled to announce that the last number would be played by the famous master composer Franz Liszt. Her concert was a great success because she knew that he was there and that he would have the last number in her program. She played as she had never played before. That's what the psalmist meant when he wrote Psalm 98:1. God is with us now and he will have the last word. Since that is true, let us sing to the LORD a new song.

We can do more than apologize. We can play a new song. We can use our gifts to glorify our Master. We have been blessed by the forgiveness that Christ offers from the cross. He turns to us and says, "Can you do more than apologize? Can you play?" If we say "yes" and do our best, we put our gifts to work for God and others are blessed. That is true stewardship, an attitude of gratitude expressed by how we serve God and other people. That's a new song. To sing a new song to the LORD means changing from self-centeredness to God-centeredness. It means using our gifts to serve God. Most of all, it means recognizing that God rules over us.

The attitude of gratitude means that we recognize that God has dominion over us. This is the heart of the Jewish enthronement ceremony. This is the one thing needful and the hardest thing of all. It is a small matter to turn to God and expect him to give answers to our problems in a way we think he should. It is another thing all together to turn to God as Lord of our lives and submit to his will, which is the theme of the annual enthronement celebration in which this psalm was used. Submission to the Lord as God is the new song to which Psalm 98:1 points.

A New Song

I recently learned a praise song which stirred my soul.

To God be the glory.
To God be the glory.
To God be the glory.
For the things he has done.

By his blood he has saved me.
By his power he has raised me.
To God be the glory.
For the things he has done.

This song has haunted me ever since I first heard it. It is simple, yet profound. It carries the message of salvation. It is a way to sing to the Lord a new song for the marvelous thing he has done in bringing salvation through his cross.

Learning new praise music is a way to fulfill this Word from God in Psalm 98:1, but the meaning of "a new song" is much deeper than learning new music. The Word from God for today has to do with attitude. The "new song" is a change of attitude from griping to gratitude, from self-centeredness to service of the living God who is our LORD.

This is the greatest discovery that anyone can make. Some people never make this discovery. Some people make the discovery early in life, some later in life. Some make the discovery of the attitude of gratitude for what God has done, forget it for a time, then rediscover the greatest news that people have ever come to know. Whenever the gospel is preached, people have an opportunity to discover or rediscover the secret which integrates life and gives us life over death.

Isaiah, the prophet, made this discovery. He wrote:

See, the former things have taken place, and new things
I declare; before they spring into being I announce them
to you." Sing to the LORD a new song, his praise from
the ends of the earth, you who go down to the sea, and
all that is in it, you islands, and all who live in them.
— Isaiah 42:9-10

155

The author of Revelation made this discovery too. He wrote:

> *Then I saw a new heaven and a new earth, for the first heaven and the first earth had passed away, and there was no longer any sea. I saw the Holy City, the new Jerusalem, coming down out of heaven from God, prepared as a bride beautifully dressed for her husband. And I heard a loud voice from the throne saying, "Now the dwelling of God is with men, and he will live with them. They will be his people, and God himself will be with them and be their God. He will wipe every tear from their eyes. There will be no more death or mourning or crying or pain, for the old order of things has passed away." He who was seated on the throne said, "I am making everything new!" Then he said, "Write this down, for these words are trustworthy and true."*
> — Revelation 21:1-5

When we look at the cross of Christ, and Jesus dying there to give us new life, we discover the secret which we were created to know. We enthrone God and confess, "Jesus is LORD to the glory of God."

Sir James Simpson was the discoverer of the anesthetic property of chloroform. It was a great discovery which changed the way surgeries would be done thereafter. A young student once asked Simpson what his greatest discovery was. This renowned scientist quickly replied, "The greatest discovery I ever made was when I realized what sin really is and what a hold it had on me." "But," said the student, "you have made so many positive scientific discoveries ... That 'sin stuff' sounds so negative, so discouraging, so depressing." "Quite the contrary," said Simpson. "Until I understood how deeply sin affects everything I do; until I understood the coercive, manipulative nature of sin; until I truly understood the depth of it; only then could I begin to understand the freedom and new life offered by Jesus Christ."

Have you made this discovery? If not, isn't it time to stop procrastinating and embrace Christ as LORD today? If you have made this discovery, you too will want to enthrone God as LORD and "Sing to the LORD a new song, for he has done marvelous things."

Questions For Your Meditation
Or Group Discussion

1. What does "Sing to the Lord a new song" (Psalm 98:1) mean to you?

2. What was Granger Westberg's insight?

3. "Can you do more than apologize?" Franz Liszt asked. What did he mean?

4. What is the greatest discovery a person can make according to Sir James Simpson?

Chapter 17

Your Word Is A
Lamp For My Feet

Oh, how I love your law! I meditate on it all day long.
Your commands make me wiser than my enemies, for
they are ever with me. I have more insight than all my
teachers, for I meditate on your statutes. I have more
understanding than the elders, for I obey your precepts.
I have kept my feet from every evil path so that I might
obey your word. I have not departed from your laws,
for you yourself have taught me. How sweet are your
words to my taste, sweeter than honey to my mouth! I
gain understanding from your precepts; therefore I hate
every wrong path. Your word is a lamp to my feet and a
light for my path.   — Psalms 119:97-105

* * *

Psalm 119 is the longest Psalm in the Bible. It has 176 verses and 22 stanzas, each with eight verses, all of which begin with the same letter of the alphabet. Each stanza begins with the appropriate letter in the Hebrew alphabet, in order. One theme runs through all the verses and stanzas —praise for the law of God. The psalmist loves the law.

At the time of his writing this psalm, there were two parties in Judaism: (1) the devout, loyal worshipers of the LORD who loved the law of God and tried to follow it, and (2) the arrogant, stubborn evildoers who were Jews in name only and disregarded the law of God. The psalmist embraced the first group and scorned the second.

For the psalmist the word of God is the law. For Christians the word of God includes the gospel of salvation in Jesus Christ.

In both cases, God's word is a lamp for our feet and a light for our paths.

Love Of The Law

The psalmist loves the law. "Oh, how I love your law! I meditate on it all day long" (Psalm 119:97). When he thinks about the law, he realizes that it is the sweetest thing of all. "How sweet are your words to my taste, sweeter than honey to my mouth" (Psalm 119:103). When he thinks about his life, he realizes that the law of God has guided him and will guide him in the future. "Your word is a lamp to my feet and a light for my path" (Psalm 119:105).

The psalmist teaches that the law of God is eternal. It is neither a passing fancy, nor merely a human opinion. The psalmist writes: "Your word, O LORD, is eternal; it stands firm in the heavens" (Psalm 119:89). This teaching flies right in the face of the modern tendency to think of the commands of God in terms of ethical relativism.

Ethical relativism permeates our culture today. In our schools the idea of absolute truth is regarded as foolishness. Young people, be careful of the argument which trivializes the law of God in the name of tolerance: "You have your standards; I have mine. There are no absolute standards! If you think that sex outside of marriage is okay, then it is okay for you. If lying is necessary, then do it. There is no absolute standard." The Bible says that God's word is an absolute standard. God's word is true no matter how many or how few people believe it. God's standards, the Ten Commandments, are true yesterday, today, and forever. These are not the Ten Suggestions, but the Ten Commandments. Break them and you will be broken by them. Love them, meditate on them day and night, and you will find a reliable guide for your life.

A modern spiritual song based on Psalm 1 describes what happens when you love the law of God:

> *I will delight in the law of the LORD,*
> *I will meditate on it day and night.*
> *Then like a tree firmly planted I will be*
> *Grounded in your Word.*

160

Blessed is the one who follows the way of the LORD.
Blessed is the one.

When you believe in the law of God, you are like a tree planted by the living waters. You are fed. You grow. You flourish. You are blessed. When you relativize the law and set up your own law, you shrivel up and die like a tree planted in the desert with no source of life. Ethical relativism has never worked. It will never work. God's law is eternal. Every time you break God's law, you are broken by it.

A little boy brought a rabbit to school for show and tell. One student asked, "Is it a boy or a girl rabbit?" There was much discussion among the students. One little girl had a bright idea, "Let's vote on it," she said. There are some things which are not determined by majority vote. Right and wrong, as described in the Ten Commandments, is unchangeable. Sex outside of marriage is wrong. Period. Lying is wrong. Period. Idolatry is wrong. Period. Using God's name in profanity is wrong. Period.

A friend of mine who worked in the construction trade once described the misuse of God's name in modern life like this: "Contrary to popular opinion, God's last name is not damn." Taking God's name in vain is wrong. Period.

The psalmist teaches that the law of God serves as a guide for our immediate and long-term future. That is what he means when he says: "Your word is a lamp for my feet and a light for my path." Do you have some immediate decisions to be made? Consult God's law to help you determine whether the course of action you are contemplating is right or wrong. God's word is a lamp for your next steps.

Do you have some long-term plans? God's word is also a light for the path ahead. Consult the word to determine the way God wants you to go. The law of God can serve as the basis for determining if the course you are contemplating is wrong or right. As a Christian, you can also ask what Jesus would do. Many young Christian people today are wearing bracelets with the letters "W.W.J.D.?" on them. "What would Jesus do?"

Love Of The Gospel

As Christians we not only have love for the law of God, but the love of the gospel of Jesus Christ as the way to determine what we should do. The gospel is God's good news that in Christ our sins are covered and that we have access to forgiveness through true repentance. God's word is a lamp for our feet and a light for our path. The word of God is revealed in the New Testament. The Old Testament word is primarily law. The New Testament word is primarily gospel. In both Testaments, the word is eternal and serves as a guide for the future. For Christians, this word of God takes three forms.

First and foremost, Jesus himself is the word of God. What would Jesus want me to do about the immediate decisions I face? He is a lamp for my feet. What would Jesus have me do about the future plans I make? He is a light for my path. Jesus is the living word of God.

The Bible says:

> *In the beginning was the Word, and the Word was with God, and the Word was God. He was with God in the beginning. Through him all things were made; without him nothing was made that has been made. In him was life, and that life was the light of men. The light shines in the darkness, but the darkness has not understood it ... The Word became flesh and made his dwelling among us. We have seen his glory, the glory of the One and Only, who came from the Father, full of grace and truth.*
> — John 1:1-14

The book of Hebrews says, "Jesus Christ is the same yesterday and today and forever" (Hebrews 13:8).

Jesus is God's eternal, living word, not just one religious teacher among many. Jesus is the guide for life, the lamp for my feet and the light for my path. He shows me where to go and what to do. That's why we love to tell his story.

> *I love to tell the story of unseen things above,*
> *Of Jesus and his glory, of Jesus and his love.*

I love to tell the story, because I know it's true;
It satisfies my longings as nothing else would do.

I love to tell the story: how pleasant to repeat
What seems, each time I tell it, more wonderfully sweet!
I love to tell the story, for some have never heard
The message of salvation from God's own holy Word.
(Refrain)

I love to tell the story, for those who know it best
Seem hungering and thirsting to hear it like the rest.
And when, in scenes of glory, I sing the new, new song,
I'll sing the old, old story that I have loved so long.
(Refrain)

Refrain:
I love to tell the story; I'll sing this theme in glory
And tell the old, old story of Jesus and his love.
— Katherine Hankey

Second, the Bible is the written word of God. A student of the great nineteenth century preacher Charles Spurgeon once asked him, "How do you defend the Bible?" He smiled and answered with a question: "How would you defend a lion? Let it loose. It will defend itself."

The problem today is that the word of God is not let loose in the lives of most people. Today, most people are biblically illiterate. People often judge the Bible with little or no knowledge of it. They dismiss it without ever knowing what it is about. One biblically ignorant teenager said, "I don't believe in the Bible. It is just the opinion of men who lived a long time ago. I trust my desires and willpower more than I trust the Bible." Son, I would not trust you as far as I could throw you.

At King of Glory Lutheran Church we set as our highest priority Bible-centered ministries. We tried to teach the word of God as a biblical corrective for a world gone astray. The written word of God is rich and full of promises, one of which is "What a man sows, that shall he reap." Another is "He who believes (in Christ) has eternal life." You can count on these truths. Period. God's promises are eternal. They serve as a guide for your future and mine.

Third, the preaching of the word is the word of God. If I thought that all I was doing in preaching was giving a lecture on a religious subject based on my schooling and reading, I would quit today. The preaching of the gospel of salvation through Jesus Christ is the word of God. The gospel changes peoples' lives.

Saint Paul puts it this way:

> *Everyone who calls on the name of the Lord will be saved. How, then, can they call on the one they have not believed in? And how can they believe in the one of whom they have not heard? And how can they hear without someone preaching to them? And how can they preach unless they are sent?* — Romans 10:13b-15a

We hear that there is a shortage of pastors today, that young people are choosing professions where they can make a lot of money and that being a minister is not one of these professions. There is a certain truth in that, but we do not just need more preachers today; we need more preachers who preach salvation through Jesus Christ, the eternal Son of God. We do not need more pastors; we need more pastors who teach the Bible truths as eternal guidelines for living.

The preaching of the gospel is one of the forms which the word of God takes. It is a noble calling, not a money-making profession. The world needs the gospel, the biblical corrective for human foolishness. The world needs heralds of the gospel.

That Psalm 119 is the longest Psalm in the Bible, and that there are 172 verses and 22 stanzas in Psalm 119 is interesting information. That this psalm points us to the way of salvation is more than interesting. It makes an eternal difference in your life and mine. "Your word is a lamp for my feet and a light for my path."

Questions For Meditation
Or Group Discussion

1. The psalmist loved the law of God. Some people hate the law of God. Why?

2. Where have you seen evidence of ethical relativism in our society?

3. The word of God takes three forms for Christians. What are they and how do people experience communication from God through them?

   1)

   2)

   3)

Chapter 18

I Will Lift Up My
Eyes To The Hills

I lift up my eyes to the hills — where does my help come from? My help comes from the LORD, the Maker of heaven and earth. He will not let your foot slip — he who watches over you will not slumber; indeed, he who watches over Israel will neither slumber nor sleep. The LORD watches over you — the LORD is your shade at your right hand; the sun will not harm you by day, nor the moon by night. The LORD will keep you from all harm — he will watch over your life; the LORD will watch over your coming and going both now and forevermore. — Psalms 121:1-8

* * *

We focus here on help: Psalm 121:1-2 says: "I will lift my eyes to the hills — where does my help come from? My help comes from the LORD, the Maker of heaven and earth."

Many of us love hills and mountains. Many vacation spots include hills and mountains which remind us of God, just as the psalmist was reminded of the Creator when he looked unto the hills.

This is a psalm for travelers, not just travelers on vacation, but travelers through life. Psalm 121:1-8 is a reminder that God is our Creator and our Watchman throughout the journey called life.

God Is Our Creator

The Psalmist says, "I lift my eyes to the hills — where does my help come from? My help comes from the LORD, Maker of heaven and earth" (Psalm 12:1-2).

167

The psalmist looks to the mountains and remembers his Maker. In this journey through life, many things change, but there is one thing that is stable like a mountain, God, our Creator.

Where should I look for help in my need? The Brandt paraphrase is a helpful reminder of our Maker:

> *The answer to my problems and the fulfillment of my needs must come from God Himself, from Him who created skies and mountains and man to dwell in their midst. He is a great God who knows our every desire whose watchful eye is upon us night and day. We can make no move without His knowledge. His concern for His children is constant; His love for them is eternal.[27]*

Think back on your life and remember that God has been there to help you. It is good to remember our Creator in the midst of all the changes we experience in life. A friend recently gave me an analysis of the last sixty years, which gives some perspective on the importance of having a relationship with our Creator who gives us stability in the midst of change.

Nostalgia

If you are near sixty, you have been witness to more changes — good and bad — than any other generation from Adam and Eve on. Wow! What a time you have lived. Consider the following:

Consider the changes! We were born before television, before penicillin, before polio shots, frozen foods, Xerox, plastics, contact lenses, Frisbees and the Pill.

We were before radar, credit cards, split atoms, laser beams, and ball point pens, before pantyhose, dishwashers, clothes dryers, electric blankets, air conditioners, drip-dry clothes ... and before man walked on the moon.

We got married first and then lived together. How quaint can you be?

In our time, closets were for clothes, not for "coming out of."

We thought fast food was what you ate during Lent,
and Outer Space was the back of the Strand Theater.
We were before house-husbands, gay rights, com-
puter dating, dual-careers, and commuter marriages.
We were before day-care centers, group therapy and
nursing homes. We never heard of FM radio, tape decks,
electric typewriters, artificial hearts, word processors,
yogurt and guys wearing earrings. For us, time-shar-
ing meant togetherness ... not computers or condomini-
ums; a "chip" meant a piece of wood; hardware meant
hardware and software wasn't even a word.

In 1940, "Made in Japan" meant junk and the term
"making out" referred to how you did on your exams. Piz-
zas, "McDonalds" and instant coffee were unheard of.

We hit the scene when there were 5 and 10 cent
stores, where you bought things for five and ten cents.
Sanders or Williams sold ice cream cones for a nickel
or a dime. For one nickel you could ride a street car,
make a phone call, buy a Pepsi or enough stamps to
mail one letter and two postcards. You could buy a new
Chevy coupe for 600 dollars, but who could afford one
— a pity too, because gas was eleven cents a gallon.

In our day, cigarette smoking was fashionable,
grass was mowed, coke was a cold drink, and pot was
something you cooked in. Rock music was Grandma in
a rocking chair humming a lullaby, aids were helpers
in the Principal's office and mother was one word ...
not two!

We were certainly not before the difference between
the sexes were discovered, but we were surely before
the sex change — we made do with what we had. And
we were the last generation that was so dumb as to
think you needed a husband to have a baby!

No wonder we were so confused and there is such
a generation gap today! But we survived. What better
reason to celebrate!

— Anonymous

As we think back on the past and the changes which have oc-
curred, it is good to look at the mountains and remember that God,
our Creator is strong and stable. He has been our steady, strong and

stabilizing LORD in the past. As we look forward to the future, the mountains remind us of God, the watchman, guardian and guide.

We survived the ordeals of the past because our strong God has been present. He has been there through all the changes of our lives. He has been there for more than the last sixty years. He has been there from the beginning of time. God is our Creator, the Maker of heaven and earth. A glimpse of the hills tells me so!

God Is Our Watchman, Guardian, And Guide

God is our watchman. Verses 3 and 4 put it this way: "He will not let your foot slip — he who watches over you will not slumber; indeed, he who watches over Israel will neither slumber nor sleep." It is not enough that we believe that God has been with us in the past. We want to know if he will be there in the future. "Yes," says the psalmist, "you can count on him as a watchman who never slumbers."

Even while we sleep, God will watch for our enemies. In the dark desert from which this psalm comes, God stays alert to all our enemies. Jesus said, "I am the door of the sheep." That means, as our shepherd at night, he literally lays his body down as the door of the sheep-fold, keeping us from foolishly going astray and keeping the beasts of the desert from getting in. What a watchman!

God is also our guardian. He literally fights for us, day and night. Verses 5 and 6 put it this way: "The LORD watches over you — the LORD is your shade at your right hand; the sun will not harm you by day, nor the moon at night."

The Brandt paraphrase or verses 5 and 6 puts it this way: "He does care for you, and he will fight with you against the enemies of your soul."[28]

Psalm 23 puts it this way, "Your rod and your staff, they protect me." The rod of the shepherd is a baseball bat-like club used by which the shepherd to beat off the enemies of his sheep. Day and night the rod is used to club the beasts which would devour us. The staff is used day and night to keep the sheep together as a flock and to rescue the lost sheep.

Can the scorching sun give us sunstroke? No, the LORD provides shade. Can the dangers of the dark capture us? No, the LORD overcomes them. He fights for us as a guardian.

The LORD is not only our watchman and guardian. He is also our guide: "The LORD will keep you from all harm — he will watch over your life; the LORD will watch over your coming and going both now and forever" (Psalm 121:7-8).

The Brandt paraphrase puts it this way: "Whether you be coming or going, he knows the course you take, and he will go before you."[29]

The LORD, our guide, knows the wilderness. He knows where he is going. He doesn't just go along, he leads the way. The rich imagery of both the Old Testament and the New Testament helps us in this respect.

In the Old Testament, God is pictured as the guide for the journey from Egypt to the Promised Land. This guide goes before his people as a pillar of cloud by day and a pillar of fire by night. God is not just with us in the wilderness of life. He is out in front, the avant guard and guide who leads the way.

In the New Testament, Jesus is pictured as the good shepherd. A good shepherd leads his flock. Without him the sheep get lost and die, but if they follow his lead, the shepherd will get them to the Land called Promise.

In the New Testament, Jesus is also pictured as the Suffering Servant. That means that he takes our suffering upon himself. It passes through him before it reaches us. Jesus' death on the cross means that my coming into any situation or going out of any situation is intimately known to him. I am never alone with my suffering. "I will not leave you bereft," Jesus said. There are resources in him to deal with all enemies, even death itself. There is nothing in life or death which I need go through alone. Jesus is my strong guide through life and death.

God our Creator, has been with me in the past. Jesus is with me in the present and the future as watchman, guardian and guide. Jesus, the Suffering Servant, died on the cross on a hill outside Jerusalem called Calvary.

Look at the hill called Calvary and say: "I lift my eyes to the hills — where does my help come from? My help comes from the LORD, the Maker of heaven and earth."

Questions For Meditation
Or Group Discussion

1. Do you remember anything about hills and mountains from your childhood?

2. Do you love hills and mountains? Why or why not?

3. What do the following words mean to you?

    1) Watchman

    2) Guardian

    3) Guide

Chapter 19

I Wait For The Lord

I wait for the LORD, my soul waits, and in his word I hope; my soul waits for the LORD more than the watchmen for the morning, more than the watchmen for the morning. O Israel, hope in the LORD! For with the LORD there is steadfast love, and with him is plenteous redemption. And he will redeem Israel from all his iniquities. — Psalm 130:5-8, RSV

* * *

I invite you to read Psalm 130:5 as your memory verse for each day this week. It will enrich your life. "I wait for the Lord, my soul waits, and in his word I hope."

Waiting Is Difficult

In our age of instant gratification, we find it very hard to wait. To try to avoid waiting, we have drive-in restaurants, drive-in cleaners, and drive-in movies, all designed to get us what we want when we want it. In Florida there is even a drive-in funeral home where you drive up to a window, look at the deceased, honk your sympathy, and drive on. Fast food, fast cars, and fast sex are designed to pander to our desire for instant gratification. Yet, we cannot avoid waiting.

We wait for people to answer the phone. We wait at traffic lights. We wait in line for car license registrations. We wait to have our vehicles fixed. We wait for babies to come and for suffering loved ones to die. We wait in doctors' offices and for lab reports. We wait at hospitals for news about how surgery has turned out. We wait for letters from loved ones far away. We wait for loved ones to arrive.

Waiting is difficult. We tend to be impatient, some more, some less. One woman sensing her problem of impatience, prayed, "Lord, give me patience and give it to me right now."

Many of us can identify with Ben Patterson who begins his book, *Waiting,* with this comment:

> *I hate to wait. My image of hell is an eternity of stand-ing in line, waiting in the lobby of some Kafkaesque bureaucracy. My teeth clench, my blood pressure rises, my field of vision narrows and my temper erupts. I've embarrassed my wife, my friends and myself at things I've said and done when I've had to wait. And I'm forced to do it several times a week — at supermarket check-out counters, in freeway traffic snarls, at the bank, and in the fast-food drive through. These daily waits never fail to try my nerves.* [30]

Some situations of waiting might be called acute waiting:

> *... the waiting of a childless couple for a child; the wait-ing of a single person for marriage or whatever is next; the waiting of the chronically ill for health or death; the waiting of the emotionally scarred for peace; the waiting of men and women in dead-end careers for a breakthrough; the waiting of unhappy marriages for relief or redemption or escape; the waiting of students to get on with life; the waiting of the lonely to belong.* [31]

Waiting is the common denominator of us all. Some who are rich and powerful cut through some of the red tape of life and find ways around some of the waiting, but all of us have to deal with the problem and the challenge of waiting. Waiting is generally a negative experience, but there is one kind of waiting described in the Bible which is good. It is called *waiting for God.*

The psalmist of old speaks of this kind of waiting — waiting for the LORD: "I wait for the LORD, my soul waits, and in his word I hope" (Psalm 130:5).

Waiting For The Lord Is Rewarding

Waiting for the Lord means at least three things: *help, humility,* and *hope.* First, when we wait for the LORD, we realize our need for help with our sins and our suffering. The context for waiting for the LORD in Psalm 130 is the realization of a need for help. We do not know why, but we do know that the psalmist got in touch with his sin and realized what his iniquities were doing to separate him from God. He saw his need for help with his offenses.

In Psalm 130:1-4, the psalmist writes:

> *Out of the depths I cry to thee, O LORD! Lord, hear my voice! Let thy ears be attentive to the voice of my supplications! If thou, O LORD, shouldst mark iniquities, Lord, who could stand? But there is forgiveness with thee, that thou mayest be feared.*

It is hard to admit that we are helpless. It is hard to admit that we have done wrong. It is difficult to face the fact that we are out of control and that we need God, but that is the school of life in which we can learn the greatest lesson of all — that God is willing to help us with our sins. "There is forgiveness with thee ..." the psalmist wrote, but before discovering it, he had to go out of control and learn to depend on God. That dependence is called waiting for the LORD.

God helps us with our need for forgiveness of sins. He also helps us with our suffering.

The psalmist cries out of his suffering: "Out of the depths, I cry to thee, O Lord" (Psalm 130:1). From the depths of suffering he learned a new dependence on God. We don't know what suffering the psalmist was experiencing, but we know that he was suffering greatly. Perhaps it was a cry for help from spiritual, psychological and physical suffering which caused him to cry out for help, to cry out from the depths. This is often the case with us as well. We too need help with our sins and suffering. But we need more. If we just discover our helplessness, we will stay far short of the full meaning of waiting for the Lord. We may wind up in the never-never land of hopelessness.

Second, when we wait for the LORD, we have to learn humility. Humility means turning from the realization of our helplessness to someone who is stronger than we are. The psalmist puts it this way: "My soul waits for *the LORD*" (Psalm 130:5).

Several friends who are recovering alcoholics have told me that they did not start on the path to health until they confessed that they were helpless in their struggle against their illness and then turned to God for help. That turn is possible because God turned to us through Jesus Christ.

Saint Paul describes our need for discovering our helplessness and our need to depend on what Christ has done: "While we were yet *helpless*, at the right time Christ died for the ungodly" (Romans 5:6 RSV).

Turning to Christ who died for us is an act of humility. On the cross, Christ did for us what we could not do for ourselves. He died for us to give us help while we are helpless. He died to give us what we cannot accomplish, the forgiveness of our sins.

Humility means not only realizing our helplessness, but turning to someone higher than ourselves to resolve our sin and suffering. Just to realize our helplessness against sin and suffering may leave us in the never-never land of despair. We must turn in humility to the One who can help us.

Ben Patterson describes what humility means this way: "Humility is not a low view of oneself, it is simply a clear view of oneself in relation to others and above all God."[32]

Saint Paul describes what happens when we humbly turn to God with our sin and suffering:

> *... We rejoice in our sufferings, knowing that suffering produces endurance, and endurance produces character, and character produces hope, and hope does not disappoint us, because God's love has been poured into our hearts through the Holy Spirit which has been given to us....* — Romans 5:3-5, RSV

Consider this insight about humility:

Look at it this way. Waiting for God means being forged into the person God wants us to be. ... At least as important as the things we wait for is the work God wants to do in us as we wait.[33] *Waiting is not just the thing we do until we get what we hope for. Waiting is part of the process of becoming what we hope for.*[34]

Waiting for the LORD means humbly trusting him for forgiveness and in times of suffering.

Third, when we wait for the LORD, we discover the best thing for all: hope. Hope is what can happen when we realize we are helpless with our sins and suffering and then humbly turn our problems over to the LORD.

Waiting for God means hope. The psalmist says: "In his word, I hope" (Psalm 130:5). He also says, "O Israel, hope in the LORD! For with the LORD there is steadfast love, and with him is plenteous redemption" (Psalm 130:7). Waiting for the LORD means discovering God is redemption which gives us hope.

This kind of waiting with hope can result in renewal. Isaiah 40:30-31 describes renewal and hope this way:

Those who wait for the LORD shall renew their strength,
they shall mount up on wings like eagles, they shall run
and not be weary, they shall walk and not faint.

The context of these words from Isaiah 40 was the Babylonian Captivity of the Jews in 586 B.C. They had been taken captive by the Babylonian King Nebuchadnezzar. After many years of suffering for their sins, God returned them to their homeland. The prophecy of Isaiah was that their learning to wait for the LORD meant hope for the future. They crossed the desert wilderness on their journey home "on the wings of eagles" with the protection of God.

In our day of instant gratification where we don't want to wait for anything, it is good for us to learn to wait for the LORD and thus renew our strength and find the focus of our hope. Howard Thurmons describes the hope which emerges from humility before God.

TO HIM that waits, all things reveal themselves, provided that he has the courage not to deny in the darkness what he has seen in the light.

Waiting is a window opening on many landscapes. For some waiting means the cessation of all activity when energy is gone and exhaustion is all that the heart can manage. It is the low slow panting of the spirit. There is no will to will — "spent" is the word. There is no hope, there is no sense of anticipation or even awareness of a loss of hope. Perhaps even the memory of function itself has faded. There is now and before — there is no after.

For some, waiting is a time of intense preparation for the next leg of the journey. Here at last comes a moment when forces can be realigned and a new attack upon an old problem can be set in order. Or it may be a time of reassessment of all plans and of checking past failures against present insight. It may be the moment of the long look ahead when the landscape stretches far in many directions and the chance to select one's way among many choices cannot be denied.

For some, waiting is a sense of disaster of the soul. It is what Francis Thompson suggests in the line: "Naked I wait Thy love's uplifted stroke!" The last hiding place has been abandoned because even the idea of escape is without meaning. Here is no fear, no panic, only the sheer excrucation of utter disaster. It is a kind of emotional blackout in the final moment before the crash — it is the passage through the Zone of Treacherous Quiet.

For many, waiting is something more than all of this. It is the experience of recovering balance when catapulted from one's place. It is the quiet forming of a pattern of recollection in which there is called into focus the fragmentary values from myriad encounters of many kinds in a lifetime of living. It is to watch a gathering darkness until all light is swallowed up completely without the power to interfere or bring a halt. Then to continue one's journey in the darkness with

ones' footsteps guided by the illumination of remem-
bered radiance is to know courage of a peculiar kind
— the courage to demand that light continue to be light
even in the surrounding darkness. To walk in the light
while darkness invades, envelops, and surrounds is to
wait on the Lord. This is to know the renewal of strength.
This is to walk and faint not.[35]

A hymn writer who learned to wait for the LORD describes
the hope which emerges this way:

My hope is built on nothing less
than Jesus' blood and righteousness;
No merit of my own I claim,
But wholly lean on Jesus' name.
On Christ, the solid rock, I stand;
All other ground is sinking sand.

… His oath, his covenant, his blood
Sustain me in the raging flood;
When all supports are washed away,
He then is all my hope and stay.
On Christ, the solid rock, I stand;
All other ground is sinking sand.

— Edward Mote

Our Bible verse Psalm 130:5, can help us make this spiritual journey to hope: "I wait for the LORD, my soul waits, and in his word
I hope."

Questions For Meditation
Or Group Discussion

1. What are the two kinds of waiting?

2. Comment on these three words:

   1) Help

   2) Humility

   3) Hope

Chapter 20

When God Seems Far Away

Lord, you have searched me out and known me.
— Psalm 139:1, RSV

*　*　*

Lord, You Search For Me

Sometimes God seems far away. We turn to him in a time of need, and he doesn't seem to be there. This is called "the dark night of the soul." Many sincere believers have experienced this "dark night of the soul" when God seems to be absent. Jesus himself experienced it on the cross when he said, "My God, my God, why have you forsaken me?"

Ezekiel, the prophet, says that Israel was turned into a field of dead, dry bones. Ever feel that way? Like you are dead inside, forsaken, alone, and hopeless?

When you feel forsaken, it is a good time to turn to Psalm 139:1. At such times it is good to assert with the ancient psalmist this basic truth about our heavenly Father: "Lord, you have searched me out and known me."

The feeling of forsakenness means that I feel alone, abandoned, separated. Psalm 139:1 assures me that I am never alone, because God, my Father, seeks me out. Life is like a race. Sometimes we get very tired and almost give up. That is the time to remember our heavenly Father and the haunting voice, "I am with you; I am for you" which stands behind this memorable line from Psalm 139.

The Leslie Brandt paraphrase of Psalm 139:1-11 is a helpful reminder that God, our Father, is seeking us out and searching for us.

O God, You know me inside and out, through and
through. Everything I do, every thought that flits through
my mind, every step I take, every plan I make, every
word I speak ...
    There is no way to escape You, no place to hide. If
I ascend to the heights of joy, You are there before me.
If I am plunged into the depths of despair, You are there
to meet me. I could fly to the other side of our world
and find You there to lead the way. I could walk into the
darkest of nights, only to find You there to lighten its
dismal hours. [36]

When life seems too tough for us to handle and we turn to
God, we sometimes feel that he, too, has deserted us. Feelings can
really fool us. Demonic forces are at work trying to separate us
from God. It is good to remind ourselves that in the dark night of
the soul God brings light. The heavenly Father seeks us out.
    There is no place to flee from our heavenly Father. He isn't
absent. It just feels that way sometimes. As Francis Thompson puts
it, God is the hound of heaven searching us out.

The Hound Of Heaven
I fled Him down the nights and down the days;
I fled Him down the arches of the years;
I fled Him down the labyrinthine ways
of my mind and in the mist of tears.
I hid from him ... under running
laughter ...
From those strong feet that followed,
followed after.

But, with unhurrying chase,
and unperturbed pace,
Deliberate speed, majestic instancy,
They beat — and a voice beat,
More instant than the feet —
"All things betray thee who betrayest Me."
           — Francis Thompson

God, the "Hound of Heaven," searches us out and knows us. God is our heavenly Father who seeks to love and support us in every way possible.

The two most-remembered Father's Day gifts I have received have the theme of our heavenly Father seeking us, finding us, and affirming us. The first came in 1989. The second, which I will mention later, came in 1995 from one of our daughters.

In June 1989, a few days before Father's Day, I got a phone call from Chicago. The message was "Harry was baptized today." Harry was 76 years old at the time. He had been stubbornly resistant to the Christian faith all of his life. Our family had prayed for him regularly, but it seemed that there was no hope for him to become a Christian. Harry was a humanist, a good moral man, who did not know God. When I talked to him about it, he turned a deaf ear to the gospel of salvation through Christ

We continued to pray for him, but it felt like God wasn't listening. God seemed far away when it came to the topic of Harry. At speaking events I had asked hundreds of people to pray for Harry, winging their prayers toward Chicago, but it just did not seem that our prayers would be answered. Harry was stubbornly resistant. On June 14, 1989, all that changed. Harry confessed the faith and was baptized. That was the best Father's Day gift I have ever received. Harry, who died two years after his baptism, was my father. God searched him out and knew him.

Lord You Know Me

"Lord, you know me," the psalmist wrote (Psalm 139:1).

In Hebrew the verb "to know" is *yada. Yada* is used to describe the most intimate of relationships. The Bible says, "He went into the tent and *knew* his wife." That means intimate sexual relations took place. The same word, *yada,* is used in Psalm 46:10 to describe our relationship with God. "Be still and *know* that I am God." That verb "to know" is used here in Psalm 139:1 too: "You have searched me out and *known* me."

That God knows us means that there is help when we feel like giving up. Consider that God can overcome your mood of feeling forsaken and raise you to a new level of intimacy if you remember two things. The author of Psalm 139 considered both of these things as he contemplated the nature of God.

First, God created me. The psalmist moves to a mood of feeling personally affirmed and known by remembering his creation. The King James version of verse 14 is helpful: "I am fearfully and wonderfully made" (Psalm 139:14, KJV).

Leslie Brandt paraphrases Psalm 139:12ff like this:

> *You were present at my very conception. You guided the molding of my unformed members within the body of my mother. Nothing about me, from beginning to end, was hid from Your eyes. How frightfully, fantastically wonderful it all is!*[37]

If God made me, he knows all about me. Martin Luther puts it this way: "God created me, and all that exists."[38]

To get in touch with the importance of this verse, "Lord ... you know me," consider the intricate workings of your mind and your body. When your mind says, "wiggle," your toes wiggle. When your mind says, "move," your fingers move. When your mind says, "run," your legs run. We are fearfully and wonderfully made. Consider the eyes with which you see; the ears with which you hear; the nose with which you smell. Think about the wonders of the reproductive system which process a newborn baby. Parents of newborns marvel at the wonder of the process in which they have been allowed to participate. We are fearfully and wonderfully made!

"Lord, you know me," the psalmist cries out in wonder, thinking about creation.

Second, God personally affirms me.

The Brandt paraphrase of the end of Psalm 139 speaks of God's guidance and affirmation.

> *May Your all-knowing, everywhere-present Spirit continue to search out my feelings and thoughts. Deliver me from that which may hurt or destroy me, and guide me along the paths of love and truth.*[39]

In our Gospel lesson today, Matthew 9:9-13, Jesus said to Matthew the tax collector, "Follow me." Put your name there. Substitute your name for Matthew's, and you will hear the personal call of God across time and eternity, affirming you.

Earlier when I mentioned the best Father's Day gift I have ever received, my earthly father's coming to know the powerful, persistent love of our heavenly Father, I mentioned a second Father's Day gift — one that recently came from one of our daughter's. It is a poem by Dee Graberg called, "The Race." Let me conclude by sharing a portion of it with you.

The context is a track meet in which a father is watching his son race. The boy stumbles and falls three times and almost gives up, but the haunting memory of his father watching and affirming him, urges him on.

> *Defeat! He lay there silently*
> *— a tear dropped from his eye —*
> *There is no sense in running more;*
> *Three strikes, I'm out, why try?*
>
> *"I've lost so what is the use," he thought.*
> *"I'll live with my disgrace."*
> *But then he thought about his dad,*
> *Who, soon, he'd have to face.*
>
> *"Get up!" an echo sounded low,*
> *"Get up and take your place.*
> *You were not meant for failure here,*
> *Get up and win the race."*
>
> *"With borrowed will get up," it said,*
> *"You haven't lost at all.*
> *For winning is no more than this;*
> *To rise each time you fall."*
>
> *So far behind the others now*
> *— the most he'd ever been —*
> *Still, he gave it all he had,*
> *And ran as though to win.*

They cheered the winning runner,
As he crossed the line first place,
head high, and proud, and happy.
No falling, no disgrace.

But, when the fallen youngster
Crossed the line in last place,
The crowd gave him the greater cheer
For finishing the race.

And even though he came in last,
With head bowed low, unproud,
You would have thought he won the race
To listen to the crowd.

And to his dad, he sadly said,
"I didn't do so well."
"To me, you won!" his father said.
"You rose each time you fell."

And now when things seem dark and hard,
And difficult to face.
The memory of that little boy,
Helps me to win my race.

For all of life is like that race
With ups and downs and all,
And all you have to do to win,
Is rise each time you fall.

"Quit! Give up! You're beaten!"
They still shout in my face.
But, another voice, within me said:
"GET UP AND WIN THE RACE!"

Life is like a race. It makes all the difference in the world that our Father is cheering us on.

Questions For Meditation
Or Group Discussion

1. Is it always comfortable for us when God is searching us out? Explain!

2. What difference does it make that God affirms us?

Chapter 21

Fearfully And
Wonderfully Made

---

*You created my inmost being; you knit me together in
my mother's womb. I praise you because I am fearfully
and wonderfully made; your works are wonderful, I
know that full well.* — Psalm 139:13-14

* * *

These Psalm verses are a wake-up call. Consider the awakening to our creation and the possibility of praise.

The Awakening To How We Were Made

Psalm 139:13-14 calls us to an awakening about how we were made and who made us.

The psalmist writes: "You knit me together in my mother's womb" (Psalm 139:13b). This verse speaks to us about our Creator and the wonder of our bodies.

Dr. Paul Brand, a hand surgeon and leprosy specialist, has co-authored a book titled *Fearfully and Wonderfully Made.* Dr. Brand writes:

> *When my cells work well, I'm hardly conscious of their
> individual presence. What I feel is the composite of their
> activity known as Paul Brand. My body, composed of
> many parts, is one.*[40]

Dr. Brand is describing in modern medical terms what the ancient psalmist felt when he said: "We are fearfully and wonderfully made." Dr. Brand goes on to explain the wonder of the white cells in our bodies:

> *To combat ... threats, some of the blood's white cells are specifically targeted to one type of invader. If the body has experienced contact with a severe danger, as in a smallpox vaccination, it imprints certain white cells with a death-wish to combat that signal danger. These cells spend their lives coursing through the bloodstream, waiting, scouting. Often they are never called upon to give battle. But if they are, they hold within them the power to disarm a foreign agent that could cause the destruction of every cell in the body.*[41]

The body. Amazing! Wonderful! Awe inspiring! Consider the eyes with which you are now seeing. Dr. Brand imagines using his eyes to look at an amoebae in a microscope.

> *The amoeba has one cell. Inside my human eye, peering at him, are 107,000,000 cells. Seven million are cones, each loaded to fire off a message to the brain when a few photons of light cross them. Cones give me the full band of color awareness, and because of them I can easily distinguish a thousand shades of color. The other hundred million cells are rods, backup cells for use in low light. When only rods are operating, I do not see color (as on a moonlit night when everything looms in shades of gray), but I can distinguish a spectrum of light so broad that the brightest light I perceive is a billion times brighter than the dimmest.*[42]

The eye points us to how wonderfully we are made. So does the ear. Think about the ears with which you are currently hearing me. Or think about how the ear and brain process music.

> *I greatly enjoy another human pleasure: listening to a symphony orchestra. When I do, the chief source of what I interpret as pleasure is located inside my ear. There I*

*can detect sound frequencies that flutter my eardrums
as faintly as one billionth of a centimeter (a distance
one tenth the diameter of a hydrogen atom). This vi-
bration is transmitted into my inner ear by three bones
familiarly known as the hammer, anvil and stirrup.
When the frequency of middle C is struck on a piano,
the piston of bones in my inner ear vibrates 256 times a
second. Further in are individual cilia, comparable to
the rods and cones of the eye, that transmit specific
messages of sound to the brain. My brain combines
these messages with other factors — how well I like
classical music, how familiar I am with the piece being
played, the state of my digestion, the friends I am with
— and offers the combination of impulses in a form I
perceive as pleasure.*[43]

Consider the ear and the brain and confess with the psalmist,
"I am fearfully and wonderfully made." And this is only the beginning of the process of considering the wonders of the body God
has given us.

Dr. Brand goes on:

*The aristocrats of the cellular world are the sex cells
and nerve cells. A woman's contribution, the egg, is
one of the largest cells in the human body, its ovoid
shape just visible to the unaided eye. It seems fitting
that all the other cells in the body should derive from
this elegant and primordial structure. In great contrast
to the egg's quiet repose, the male's tiny sperm cells
are furiously flagellating tadpoles with distended heads
and skinny tails. They scramble for position as if com-
petitively aware that only one of billions will gain the
honor of fertilization.*[44]

Think about the wonders of human reproductive systems, and
the cells in our bodies by which God creates other human beings.
Words fail to describe the wonder of a sex cell. Lewis Thomas puts
it this way:

The mere existence of that cell should be one of the greatest astonishment's of the earth. People ought to be walking around all day, all through their waking hours, calling to each other in endless wonderment, talking of nothing except that cell ... If anyone does succeed in explaining it, within my lifetime, I will charter a skywriting airplane, maybe a whole fleet of them and send them aloft to write one great exclamation point after another, around the whole sky, until all my money runs out.[45]

Dr. Brand explains nerve cells like this:

The king of cells, the one I have devoted my life to studying, is the nerve cell. It has an aura of wisdom and complexity about it. Spider-like, it branches out and unites the body with a computer network of dazzling sophistication. Its axons, "wires" carrying distant messages to and from the human brain, can reach a yard in length. I never tire of viewing these varied specimens.[46]

Think about sex cells and nerve cells and confess with the psalmist: "I am fearfully and wonderfully made."

Time does not allow us to go on, but the point is well made that our bodies are filled with wonders. Yet, we so easily take our bodies for granted. Dr. Brand explains the problem of doctors not fully appreciating the body God has given us like this:

We doctors are like employees at the complaint desk of a large department store. We tend to get a biased view of the quality of the product when we hear about its aches and pains all day.

Something like that happens to all of us. We tend to take the body for granted until something goes wrong with it. More importantly, we tend to take God who made these bodies, for granted. That is why it is so important to follow the example of the psalmist and praise God for what he has created.

The Awakening To The Possibility Of Praise

The ancient psalmist wrote: "I praise you because I am fearfully and wonderfully made; your works are wonderful, I know that full well" (Psalm 39:14). This verse speaks to us about praising God.

One of our human maladies is that we take our bodies for granted. A more serious malady is that we take God for granted. That is why praise is so important. Look at three areas of praise in Psalm 139.

First, Psalm 139:1-6 teaches us to appreciate and praise God for his knowledge of us. Look at the first six verses of this psalm and be inspired to overcome that malady of taking God for granted.

> *O Lord, you have searched me and you know me.*
> *You know when I sit and when I rise; you know my*
> *thoughts from afar.*
> *You discern my going out and my lying down; you are*
> *familiar with all my ways.*
> *Before a word is on my tongue you know it completely,*
> *O Lord.*
> *You hem me in — behind and before; you have laid*
> *your hand upon me.*
> *Such knowledge is too wonderful for me, too lofty for*
> *me to retain.*

We praise God because he knows us intimately. He knows our past, present and future. We also praise him because of his never tiring effort to find us.

Second, we praise God because he seeks us out. That is a reminder about the nature of God in this psalm which can lift us from lethargy. Consider verses 7-12:

> *Where can I go from your Spirit? Where can I flee from*
> *your presence? If I go up to the heavens, you are there;*
> *if I make my bed in the depths, you are there. If I rise on*
> *the wings of the dawn, if I settle on the far side of the*
> *sea, even there your hand will guide me, your right hand*
> *will hold me fast.*

Praise God. He seeks us out wherever we go. That is the meaning of the coming of Jesus Christ. God will not let us wallow in our sins. He comes in the person of Jesus Christ to find us and save us. In Christ, God seeks us and finds us.

Third, Psalm 139:13-14 teaches us to praise God for the wonders of the body. That we are "fearfully made" means that we are in awe of what God has created. That we are wonderfully made means that we can be appreciative of the wonder of God's creation. "I praise you because I am fearfully and wonderfully made," the psalmist wrote.

Praise God who knows us.
Praise God who redeems us.
Praise God who has created us.

I praise you (Lord) because I am fearfully and wonderfully made; your works are wonderful, I know that full well" (Psalm 139:14). When I think about you Lord, my words fail me. I am undone. I cannot grasp what you have done. Such wonders are too much for me. But I rise from the dust and praise your holy name.

Questions For Meditation
Or Group Discussion

1. Think about the wonder of your body. What comes to mind?

2. Why do we praise God for our bodies?

Chapter 22

The High And The Holy One
Delivers Help And Hope

---

*Your kingdom is an everlasting kingdom, and your do-
minion endures through all generations. The LORD is
faithful to all his promises and loving toward all he has
made.* — Psalm 145:13

Praise the LORD.
Praise the LORD, O my soul.
I will praise the LORD all my life;
I will sing praise to my God as long as I live ...

Blessed is he whose help is the God of Jacob,
whose hope is in the LORD his God ...

The LORD reigns forever
your God, O Zion, for all generations.
Praise the LORD.
— Psalm 146:1-2, 5, 10

*   *   *

These verses from Psalm 145 and 146 both center on the kingdom of God. The psalmist's prayer is: "Your kingdom is an everlasting kingdom, and your dominion endures through all generations" (Psalm 145:13). The psalmist's confession is: "The LORD
reigns forever ..." (Psalm 146:10).

Both the prayer and confession center on the kingdom of God.
The kingdom of God is one of the most important terms in the
Bible. Literally, the kingdom of God means the reign or rule of

God over our lives. Our part of the kingdom is submission to God's authority, the one thing needful and the hardest thing of all.

A new Christian once told me: "Submitting my will to God was the hardest thing I have ever done. I kept thinking that if I submitted to God I would lose everything. Instead I gained more than I could ever hope for. Now I want to pass on the help and hope I received from God." This new Christian discovered the everlasting kingdom of God described in Psalms 145 and 146. He personally discovered that "The LORD reigns forever."

The High And The Holy

Psalm 145:13 helps us to re-center our lives on God through praise. "Your kingdom is an everlasting kingdom...." This prayer of submission shows us what we need to do before God. Submission: the one thing needful and the hardest thing of all, acknowledging God as the high and holy One who rules over us.

The kingdom of God is not only an important biblical concept, it is also an important concept for the church today. It is easy for the church to drift into cultural patterns which are not centered in our biblical heritage. It is essential that we get back to basics. The most basic thing of all is that we submit to the high and the holy One and pass on the help and hope which we receive from God.

Discovering the kingdom of God means submission. A simple outline of the Bible will help us get in touch with the problem of submission.

I. *Genesis 1 and 2.* God created us by his authority.
II. *Genesis 3.* Adam and Eve, representing all of us, rebel against God's authority.
III. *Genesis 4* through the end of Revelation. God works to re-establish his authority over us for our own good.

That's what the kingdom of God is all about: God seeking to help us learn to submit to his authority for our own good. God seeks to be our LORD, not because he needs our peeps of praise, but because this is the design of the universe. As we submit to God's authority, we are fulfilled. That's why the result of this submission is praise.

The problem is that we resist submitting. We insist on our way, our will, our rights. We want to promote our names and causes. We get caught in the chaos of worldly kingdoms and marginalize God's kingdom.

When we refuse to submit to God, we are bucking the *established system* of the universe. Psalm 103:19 says, "The LORD has established his throne in heaven, and his kingdom rules over all."

Jesus said, "Seek first the kingdom of God and his righteousness ..." (Matthew 6:33). Jesus wants us to be happy. That's why he wants us to get back to the most basic thing of all: submission to God.

While he was here on earth, Jesus repeatedly said in his parables, "The kingdom of God is like ..." This is the most basic thing of all: submitting to the high and holy One. The parables describe God's will and God's ways. When we tune into this station, we praise God for all that he has done.

Between Jesus' resurrection and ascension when he had only forty days to teach his apostles, Jesus taught them about the kingdom (Acts 1:3). His last words on earth have to do with the prime importance of submitting to God and teaching others about God's kingdom.

Sir James Simpson, the discoverer of the use of anesthesia in surgery, was once asked by one of his admiring students, "What was your greatest discovery?" Simpson replied: "My greatest discovery in life is that I am a great sinner who cannot help myself and that Jesus Christ is my Savior who by his work on the cross had brought hope to my life." Simpson learned the greatest secret in life: submission to the high and holy God through Jesus Christ.

The discovery of the kingdom of God results in praise. The psalmist wrote:

Praise the LORD.
Praise the LORD, O my soul.
I will praise the LORD all my life;
I will sing praise to my God as long as I live.
— Psalm 146:5

When we submit to the LORD and his control, we discern the greatest happiness possible which we express in praise.

We praise God because he is our help (Psalm 146:5). God helps us where we cannot help ourselves. He accomplishes what we cannot accomplish — bringing us back to him.

We praise God because he restores our hope.

The psalmist says, "Our hope is in the LORD our God" (Psalm 146:5). Hope is to the soul what air is to the body. The book of Hebrews speaks of hope as "the sure and steadfast anchor of the soul" (Hebrews 6:19, NRSV). We cannot live without hope. Once we discover hope in God through submission to the high and holy One, we can abound in hope, passing it on to others.

Saint Paul puts it this way: "May the God of hope fill you with all joy and peace in believing, so that you may abound in hope by the power of the Holy Spirit" (Romans 15:13, NRSV).

The person who crosses over from trying to control his or her life to submitting to the rule of God is truly blessed as the psalm says: "Blessed is he whose help is the God of Jacob, whose hope is in the LORD his God ..." (Psalm 146:5).

Passing On The Help And Hope We Receive

The kingdom of God is an everlasting kingdom. That helps us see the kingdoms of the world from a higher perspective and to see our neighbor as a person in need. If we are helped and have our hope restored, we will praise God with the psalmist and pass this help and hope on to others.

The psalmist says, "Our *help* is in the God of Jacob" (Psalm 146:5). Help does not mean that all of our problems are solved the way we expect them to be solved. When we pray to the high and holy One and praise his holy name, by submitting to God's rule, we are in touch with the power of our Maker. We have a sense of peace as we acknowledge that God is in control. We can relax and enjoy life as it was intended to be lived by the LORD who reigns forever.

When our help centers in God, we can also offer that help to others. The small act of reaching out and helping someone can have earthmoving results. A story may help to show the wonderful results of passing on help to others.

A poor Scottish farmer was out walking one day when he heard a cry coming from a nearby bog. He ran to assist a boy who was mired up to his waist, and about to drown in black muck. Extending his staff, the farmer pulled the boy out.

The next day a handsome team of horses and carriage came up to the Scotsman's small hut, and an elegantly dressed gentleman stepped out. He offered a reward to the Scotsman for saving the boy's life, but he refused it. Just then the farmer's young son came to the door. Seeing him, the nobleman made the Scotsman an offer: "Let me take your son and give him a good education. If the lad is anything like his father, he'll grow into a man you can be proud of."

The Scotsman liked this, and shook hands on the bargain.

In time, the Scotsman's son graduated from Saint Mary's Hospital Medical School in London. He later became known as Sir Alexander Fleming, the noted discoverer of penicillin. Years later the nobleman's son was stricken with pneumonia, but was saved through the use of penicillin. The nobleman was named Lord Randolf Churchill. His son was Winston Churchill who led England to victory in World War II.

— Anonymous

You never know the far-reaching affects your help can have. We help others because God has helped us. We pass hope on to others because God is a God of hope.

A new Christian who had such a hard time with submission described his journey from the kingdom of the world to the kingdom of God like this:

"Pastor, I can hardly believe how my life has changed since I committed myself to the LORD Jesus Christ. When I tried to control everything, I got hooked on alcohol, lost my wife, alienated my children and offended my friends.

"When I found new life by submitting myself to God through Jesus Christ, I found hope, the solid hope I had been missing all my life. Now I want to pass that hope on to everyone else."

Questions For Meditation
Or Group Discussion

1. Why do some people fear to submit their wills to God?

2. What is the point of the outline of the Bible in three parts?

3. What are several ways we can pass on the help and hope we receive from God?

Chapter 23

A Fistful Of Nothing

Praise the LORD. Praise God in his sanctuary; praise him in his mighty heavens. Praise him for his acts of power; praise him for his surpassing greatness. Praise him with the sounding of the trumpet, praise him with the harp and lyre, praise him with tambourine and dancing, praise him with the strings and flute, praise him with the clash of cymbals, praise him with resounding cymbals. Let everything that has breath praise the LORD. Praise the LORD. — Psalm 150:1-6

* * *

Prayer can be described in terms of an acronym ACTS: **A** — Adoration; **C** — Confession; **T** — Thanksgiving; **S** — Supplication.

Prayer consists of adoration, confession, thanksgiving and supplication, but the greatest of these, and the most neglected, is adoration. Adoration is what Psalm 150 is all about.

We can cling to the things of this world and wind up in the end with a fistful of nothing or we can open our hands, our hearts, our minds and let our voices carry praise to the throne of God in this life in anticipation of ultimate adoration in the next. Every person must make his or her own choice. "Let everything that has breath praise the LORD," the psalmist wrote. He had renounced the values and ways of this world, which eventually turn out to be nothing, in favor of what lasts — adoration of the living God expressed by praise.

A Fistful Of Nothing

Henri Nouwen, the Roman Catholic spiritual writer, says:

203

The resistance to praying is like the resistance of tightly clenched fists. This image shows a tension, a desire to cling tightly to yourself, a greediness which betrays fear.[47]

What Henri Nouwen says about the resistance to all kinds of prayers is particularly true of adoration, the praise part of prayer. In other words, if we do not fervently praise God in prayer, we are clinging to a fistful of nothing.

Nouwen goes on to tell the story of an elderly woman in a psychiatric center whose fist was so tightly fixed on something that it took two people to force open her hand. She was wild in her defense of her prized possession which she feared would be taken from her. When the workers at the psychiatric center finally got her tightly clenched fist open, it was discovered that she was clinging to a penny. The penny symbolizes a lot of disorders in our lives.

To pray, especially to pray prayers of praise, requires that we open our fists, clenched around anger, resentment, revenge, bitterness, hatred, and jealousy.

In other words, to praise God with adoration, we must release our tightly clenched fists on those things to which we cling which are killing us. These things are worth nothing but pain and sorrow, but we often cling to them as if they were valued possessions.

To be happy and have a true purpose in life, we must turn from these negative things to which we cling. We think we have a right to them because we have been hurt, but to pray, we must turn from self to God, our Creator, with open hands. Praise of God changes our focus from self to the LORD. Praise opens up our clenched fists in prayer.

Opening Up Our Hands, Hearts, And Minds

To pray means to open our hands, our hearts and our minds to God. When we pray, we discover the purpose of life. Have you ever stopped and considered the purpose of your life? *The Westminster Catechism* says, "The purpose of man is to glorify God and enjoy him forever." Purpose is a good place to focus as we look at Psalm 150, a poem/prayer of praise. The reason you are here on earth is to glorify, enjoy and praise God. Many miss their purpose altogether. The psalmist summarizes the purpose of life like this: "Praise the LORD" (Psalm 150:1).

How can we personally pick up the pulse of Psalm 150? Memorize verse one, "Praise the LORD," and repeat it for the next week at the beginning of each day. As you repeat this psalm verse each day, consider these five questions: 1) What? 2) Where? 3) Why? 4) How? And 5) Who?

What?

First, *what* is praise? The psalmist tells us to "praise the LORD," (Psalm 150:1) but what does that mean? Praise is the outflow of the soul. Praise is the power of prayer. Praise is adoration of the Almighty. Adoration centers our attitude on God in self-forgetful worship. But adoration is the most neglected aspect of prayer. Instead of adoring the Almighty and praising his name, we often get caught in the trap of murmuring, griping and grumbling. About grumpiness one woman wrote: "Today I woke up grumpy. Usually I just let him sleep in." Grumpiness in ourselves or those we love is clinging to a fistful of nothing.

The word from God in Psalm 150 is intended to turn our grumpiness into gratitude by turning our attention from self to God through adoration expressing itself as praise. That's what we have in Psalm 150: praise as a powerful prayer of adoration of the Almighty. Psalm 150:6 says, "Let everything that has breath praise the LORD." Praise is a way for all created things to glorify and enjoy God by telling God how wonderful he is.

A little boy said to his mother: "Will you play darts with me?" "Yes," said his mother. "Shall we take turns? You throw; then I'll throw?" "No," said the boy. "I'll throw the darts. You just say, 'Wonderful!'"

Praise of God is telling our Maker how wonderful we believe he is, not because he (like the little boy) needs to hear it, but because we need to say it. The song, "How Great Thou Art," is a wonderful expression of what we are called to do:

O Lord my God, when I in awesome wonder
Consider all the works thy hand hath made,
I see the stars, I hear the mighty thunder,
Thy pow'r throughout the universe displayed;
Then sings my soul, my Savior God, to thee,
How great thou art! How great thou art!
Then sings my soul, my Savior God, to thee,
How great thou art! How great thou art!

Where?

Second, *where* should we praise God? The psalmist begins his answer: "Praise God in his sanctuary ..." (Psalm 150:1a). Why do we have a church building? So that we can gather together in one place to praise the Lord in his sanctuary or holy place. But another place to praise God is mentioned in Psalm 150.

The psalmist goes on "... Praise him in his mighty heavens" (Psalm 150:1b). The praises we sing in church join us with the praises being sung by the angels in the heavens. "The heavens praise your wonders, O LORD, your faithfulness too, in the assembly of the holy ones" (Psalm 89:5). "Praise him, all his angels, praise him, all his heavenly hosts. Praise him, sun and moon, praise him, all you shining stars" (Psalm 148:2-3).

When Jesus was born, the heavenly host sang: "Glory to God in the highest and peace to his people on earth" (Luke 2:14).

Why?

Third, *why* should we praise God? The psalmist answers this question by saying: "Praise him for his acts of power; praise him for his surpassing greatness" (Psalm 150:2).

The Bible records the mighty deeds of God — creation, the exodus from Egypt, the battles against idols and the greatest deed of all, the life, death, and resurrection of Jesus. We can celebrate these mighty deeds with praise of God. We can also celebrate God's mighty deeds in our personal lives and praise him for what he has done.

Think back on your life. There have been hard times, but can't you identify the blessings of God which have come to you, even in the hardest times? Hasn't God blessed you from the beginning and

206

throughout your life? You are blessed to be a blessing. One of the ways we are a blessing is by returning praise to God with adoration.

In the Lord's Prayer in Luke 11:1-4, we read that the first thing to pray is adoration of God, by praise of his name and his kingdom.

One day Jesus was praying in a certain place. When he finished, one of his disciples said to him, "Lord, teach us to pray, just as John taught his disciples." He said to them, "When you pray, say 'Father, hallowed be your name, your kingdom come. Give us each day our daily bread. Forgive us our sins, for we also forgive everyone who sins against us. And lead us not into temptation.' "

How?

Fourth, *how* do we praise God? Of course, we can praise God in a multitude of ways — by selfless service, by words of encouragement to a needy person; by giving generously of our time and money to the cause of God and by using our gifts for God. How can we glorify and enjoy God? The psalmist concentrates on music as a major way of praising God.

Praise him with the sounding of the trumpet, praise him with the harp and lyre, praise him with tambourine and dancing, praise him with the strings and flute, praise him with the clash of cymbals, praise him with resounding cymbals. May the peoples praise you, O God; may all the peoples praise you.   — Psalm 150:3-5

Let's look more closely at the various instruments which are mentioned in Psalm 150:

1) *Trumpet (shofar)* — a ram's horn, used to call the congregation together.
2) *Harp* — David played this instrument to soothe the nerves and bring peace.
3) *Lyre* — an instrument of joy and mirth played with a pick.

4) *Drum* — beaten by hand for rhythm, often accompanied by dance to express the mode of joy and praise.
5) *Flute* — a reed tube held vertically, providing a light sense of respect and love.
6) *Clanging cymbals* — harsh and noisy; struck vertically with leather thongs, providing a sense of dynamic celebration.

Music, both instrumental and vocal, can lift us to a new level of glorifying and enjoying God. A praise song expresses the answer to the question of how to praise God. The answer is to get to higher ground.

> *I'm pressing on the upward way, new heights I'm gaining ev'ry day,*
> *Still praying as I am on-ward bound, "Lord, plant my feet on higher ground."*
> *Lord, lift me up and let me stand, By faith, on heaven's table land,*
> *A higher plane that I have found; Lord, plant my feet on higher ground.*
> *I want to live above the world, though Satan's darts at me are hurled;*
> *For faith has caught the joyful sound, the song of saints on higher ground.*
> *Lord, lift me up and let me stand, by faith, on heaven's table land,*
> *A higher plane than I have found; Lord, plant my feet on higher ground.*

Who?

Fifth, *who* should praise God? The psalmist answers the question, "Who should praise God?" "All creation," he says in a paean of praise, a great symphonic expression of adoration of the Almighty: "Let everything that has breath praise the LORD. Praise the LORD" (Psalm 150:6).

Three songs come to mind as I think about joining all creation praising God. The first song answers the question, "Who?" by saying "earth and all stars!"

Earth and all stars!
Loud rushing planets!
Sing to the Lord a new song
Oh victory!
Loud shouting army!
Sing to the Lord a new song.
He has done marvelous things.
I too will praise him with a new song.
— Herbert F. Brokering

When you sing, "I too will praise him with a new song," You add your personal choice to join creation in praising God.

The second is a children's song. All God's children should praise him. That includes you, the children of God.

Praise him, praise him, all ye little children.
God is love. God is love.
Praise him, praise him all ye little children.
God is love. God is love.

The third song is the doxology. In line two "all creatures" includes you.

Praise God from whom all blessings flow.
Praise him all creatures here below.
Praise him above ye heavenly host;
Praise Father, Son and Holy Ghost.

Who should praise God? How about you?

Questions For Meditation
Or Group Discussion

1. Outline the fivefold description of prayer from the letters:

   A

   C

   T

   S

2. Which of these is strongest in your prayer life?

3. Which of these is weakest?

4. Who is praising God at this moment?

Leaders' Guide

1. Start each session with prayer.

2. Each week (or each meeting) give out a memory verse from the next chapter to be used each day for personal devotions.

3. Use a starter question at the beginning of each session to stimulate discussion. Remember, this is a discussion group, not a class. You are a leader of growing Christians, not a teacher of information. Question one at the end of each chapter will generally serve as a good starter question for discussion.

4. Use each chapter as an outline for further discussion, and the questions at the end of each chapter as prompters for discussion.

5. End with prayer at the close of the session.

Endnotes

1. Psalm 30:11.

2. Psalm 30:11, Brandt paraphrase. Leslie Brandt, *Psalms Now* (St. Louis: Concordia, 1973), p. 48.

3. Ron Lavin, *Way To Grow! Dynamic Church Through Small Groups* (Lima, Ohio: CSS Publishing, 1997); *You Can Grow In A Small Group* (Lima, Ohio: CSS Publishing); *A Strategy For Renewal* (Board of Publication, LCA, Philadelphia, Pa.).

4. Ron Lavin, *The Advocate* (Lima, Ohio: CSS Publishing, 1999).

5. *Lutheran Book of Worship* (Minneapolis: Augsburg, 1978), Hymn #249.

6. Leslie Brandt, *Psalms Now* (St. Louis: Concordia, 1973).

7. Elmer A. Leslie, *The Psalms* (Nashville: Abingdon Press, 1956), p. 316.

8. Charles Colson, *Born Again* (Old Tappan, N.Y.: Spire Books, 1927), p. 111.

9. *Ibid.*, pp. 111-113.

10. *Ibid.*, pp. 118-130.

11. Elmer Leslie, *Psalms* (Nashville: Abingdon, 1959), pp. 286-28.

12. Leslie Brandt, *Psalms Now* (St. Louis: Concordia, 1973), p.48.

13. Adapted from Max Lucado, *Six Hours One Friday* (Multnomah Books, 1989), pp. 61-66.

14. Leslie Brandt, *Psalms Now* (St. Louis: Concordia, 1973), paraphrase of Psalm 31.

15. David Adam, Introduction to *The Cry of The Deer* (London: Triangle), pp. xi-xiv.

16. Blaise Pascal, *Penses* (Penguin Publishers, 1966), p. 48.

17. *Ibid.*, p. 72.

18. *Ibid.*, p. 434.

19. Martin Nystrom, "As The Deer."

20. Leslie Brandt, *Psalms Now* (St. Louis: Concordia, 1973), p. 82.

21. Teilhard de Chardin, *Le Milese Divin* (Collins Fontana, 1975), p. 127.

22. David Adam, *The Open Gate* (London: Triangle SPCK, 1994), p. 3.

23. *The Westminster Bible Dictionary*, p. 157.

24. Keith Miller tells this story in *The Scent of Love* (Waco, Tx.: Word Publishing, 1983), p. 8.

25. Elmer Leslie, *The Psalms* (Nashville: Abingdon Press, 1959), p. 468.

26. Charles Swindoll, *Living Above The Level of Mediocrity* (Waco, Tx.: Word Publishing, 1987), p. 80.

27. Leslie Brandt, *Psalms Now* (St. Louis: Concordia, 1973), p. 19.

28. *Ibid.*

29. *Ibid.*

30. Ben Patterson, *Waiting* (Downers Grove, Ill.: Intervarsity Press, 1989), p. 9.

31. *Ibid.*

32. *Ibid.*, p. 58.

33. *Ibid.*, p. 11.

34. *Ibid.*, p. 12.

35. From Howard Thurman's devotional, *The Inward Journey, Meditations on The Spiritual Quest!*

36. Leslie Brandt, *Psalms Now* (St. Louis: Concordia, 1973), p. 211.

37. *Ibid.*, pp. 211-212.

38. Martin Luther, *Small Catechism*, commentary on the first article of the creed.

39. *Ibid.*, p. 212.

40. Paul Brand and Philip Yancey, *Fearfully and Wonderfully Made* (Grand Rapids, Mich.: Zondervan, 1980), p.26.

41. *Ibid.*, pp. 18-19.

42. *Ibid.*, p. 22.

43. *Ibid.*, p. 24.

44. *Ibid.*, pp. 28-29.

45. Lewis Thomas, *The Medusa And The Snail* (New York: Harper and Row, 1977), pp. 155-157.

46. Brand., *op. cit.*, p. 28.

47. Henri Nouwen, *With Open Hands* (New York: Ballantine Books, N.Y., 1972), p. 3.